SAINSBURY

THE COOKING OF
THE
MIDDLE EAST

CLAUDIA RODEN

CONTENTS

Published exclusively for J Sainsbury plc
Stamford House Stamford Street
London SE1 9LL
by Martin Books
Simon & Schuster Consumer Group
Fitzwilliam House 32 Trumpington Street
Cambridge CB2 1QY

First published 1991
Text and recipes first published in
Middle Eastern Cooking, 1986

ISBN 0 85941 747 6

THE AUTHOR

Claudia Roden was born and brought up in Cairo. She finished her education in Paris and came to study art in London where she now lives. She has three grown-up children.

Her other books include *A New Book of Middle Eastern Food*, *Coffee*, *Picnic*, *Mediterranean Cookery* (based on her BBC TV series) and *The Food of Italy*.

INTRODUCTION

Inspired by fond memories of my Egyptian childhood, I started researching Middle Eastern food 26 years ago before my third child was born. After the publication of *A Book of Middle Eastern Food* I received hundreds of recipes from people who said I had forgotten to include a dish. My involvement with the subject has never ceased and when my children grew up I had the opportunity to travel and to make new discoveries; some of these have joined other classics in this book. They belong to a sensuous type of cooking where the flavours of olive oil, onion, garlic, mint and lemon and the more exotic ones of tamarind, pomegranate and the essence of flowers come into play; and where herbs are used abundantly and spices delicately.

Mishmisheya (Lamb stew with apricots, page 70)

Fasulya Pilakisi (Beans in oil, page 45)

Salata Baladi (Mixed salad Arab-style, page 27)

Herodotus wrote that Arabia was scented with spices and exhaled a marvellous sweet odour. The reason for this is that it was part of the spice route. Since early times the Middle East was the transit area and the camel and caravan route for the spices which were transported from the Far East and Central Africa to Europe. The middlemen succumbed

Borek (Little fillo savouries, page 31)

Fawakeh (Fruit, page 90)

Omi Houriya (Mashed carrot salad, page 44)

Mujadara Bil Burghul (Lentils and bulgar wheat, page 83)

Shopping

To purchase ingredients by mail order, write to:
The Green Valley
36 Upper Berkeley Street
London W1H 7PG
Tel. 071–402 7385

Note on quantities

All recipes in this book give ingredients in both metric (g, ml, etc.) and imperial (oz, pints, etc.) measures. Use either set of quantities, but not both, in any one recipe.

All teaspoons and tablespoons are level, unless otherwise stated.
1 teaspoon = a 5 ml spoon;
1 tablespoon = a 15 ml spoon.

Egg size is medium (size 3), unless otherwise stated.

to the attractions of their highly prized merchandise. Each country adopted special favourites and combinations and these characterise regional cooking today. A certain magic still surrounds the use of spices and aromatics, which are used not only for their taste but also for their medicinal, therapeutic and supposedly aphrodisiac qualities.

The countries of the Middle East have shared their past and this has given unity to their kitchen. The spread of Islam was the most important factor in the development of a gastronomic tradition comparable with that of France and China. The death of the prophet Muhammad in the year AD 632 was followed by victorious wars waged by the followers of his faith. Bedouin Arabs burst out of the Arabian Peninsula, conquered one area after another and converted it to Islam. The establishment of an enormous Islamic Empire stretching across Asia, North Africa, Spain and Sicily brought about great marriages of cooking styles and refinements in eating habits. The Turkish Ottoman empire, which expanded over an enormous territory from the fourteenth century until the twentieth, produced a new cuisine which amalgamated the old dishes with new ones.

As a result, dishes such as skewered meats cooked over charcoal; stews with vegetables and fruit; vegetables stuffed with meat or rice, or both; savoury pies made with paper-thin dough filled with cheese, spinach or meat; cold vegetables cooked in oil; omelettes thick with vegetables; meatballs; rice pilafs; milk puddings with rice; nut-filled pastries soaked in syrup and syrupy fritters have been passed around and form the theme of many a local variation.

All the countries attach great value to food. When in Turkey I asked several people why that was so. A chef in Istanbul said that it had to do with love: 'A woman shows her love by cooking well and when a man eats well he is good at making love.' In rural Anatolia a man explained: 'What gives us most pleasure in life is being hospitable, and to be hospitable you have to give food.' In the most hospitable part of the world the best food is home cooking, for life is about family and friends and pressing food on them when they visit.

With all the similarities, the cooking of the Middle East is diverse, for every city and every village has its special dishes, its favourite flavourings and makes loving use of what grows locally. They use different pots, make different fires, some cut things small while others leave them whole, some fry and some bake.

I have included recipes from Turkey, Syria and the Lebanon, Iran, Egypt, Morocco and Tunisia. Some of the dishes are classics, but many are little-known regional versions which I have picked because they are interesting, flavoursome, fresh and healthy. Most are quick to make; the more elaborate are for entertaining. On the whole I have reduced the amount of fat and sometimes used oil instead of butter.

With their happy mix of grains, pulses, seeds, nuts and vegetables it is the kind of food which fits perfectly with today's ideas of healthy eating.

REGIONAL CUISINES

Regional differences do not have much to do with national boundaries (some are relatively recent), they depend more on geography, history and local produce.

The cooking can be broadly divided into four:

IRANIAN COOKING is the oldest and many of the refined and grand dishes of the Middle East originated in ancient Persia. Its greatest influence is on the cooking of Iraq and, more surprisingly, on Morocco. It makes use of a wide range of herbs, spices and flavourings and is based on and around rice. There are, too, slowly simmered soups, stews and sauces where all kinds of vegetables, pulses (yellow split peas are favourites), nuts and remarkably fresh and dried fruits, are cooked with meat or chicken. The main herbs are dill, mint, coriander and parsley. Cinnamon, allspice, nutmeg, ginger and saffron or turmeric are used together. The sharp flavours of sour pomegranates and tamarind, dried limes and sumac are sometimes balanced with a little sweetness. Yogurt goes into many dishes.

ARAB COOKING is the cooking of Syria, the Lebanon, Jordan and Egypt. It is at its best in Syria where Aleppo is considered the great gastronomic city, and in the Lebanon (which has developed a restaurant trade, as has Turkey). It is the Lebanon, with its migrating cooks and restaurateurs, which has brought the grilled meats and appetisers of the restaurant menu to the attention of the world. The wide range of home cooking is based on wheat and rice and an abundance of vegetables. The flavours of onion and garlic, lemon, mint and fresh coriander predominate, and chick-peas and sesame paste (tahina) go into many dishes. Cinnamon is mixed with allspice, cumin with coriander and sumac and cardamom are used. Occasionally you detect tamarind or bitter oranges. Pine kernels appear often and ground almonds are used to thicken sauces.

NORTH AFRICAN (MAGHREBI) COOKING is scented and colourful and full of contrasts – hot and spicy and also sweet with sugar and honey. Couscous, of Berber origin, is the national dish. The food of Morocco is the richest and most varied – it vies with Turkish cuisine as the third best in the world after French and Chinese. There is hardly any Ottoman influence, but a great similarity with the cooking of ancient Iran and medieval Baghdad and a strong influence from Spanish Andalusia. The bourgeois cooking of Fez is the dominant cuisine. It is delicate and hardly hot; with pepper and cumin only in appetisers, and much cinnamon, saffron and ginger, mint and fresh coriander. The cuisines of Tetouan and Marrakesh are also renowned. Tunisian food, with its wonderful salads, fish and egg dishes, is underrated.

CLASSIC TURKISH COOKING was developed in Istanbul during the Ottoman Empire. Although there is great regional diversity in home cooking throughout Turkey, professional chefs offer a menu of *saray* (palace) cooking in their restaurants. They mostly come from Bolu in central Anatolia and are nearly all descended from the cooks at the sultan's kitchens. This Ottoman cuisine – with its kebabs, stuffed vegetables, savoury pies, vegetables cooked in oil, walnut sauces and plaki dishes – can be found in countries from the Danube to the tip of the Arabian Peninsula and from the Balkans to the shores of North Africa. Devoid of any extremes of taste, the natural flavour of ingredients is embellished only by herbs, olive oil, lemon juice, yogurt and a few spices – cinnamon, allspice and paprika.

INGREDIENTS
BULGAR WHEAT *Burghul* in Arabic, *bulgur* in Turkish and *pourgouri* in Cypriot, you find all these names on packets here. It is wheat which has been boiled, dried and then ground to a fine or coarse texture. It is quick and easy to use and can be served like rice, plain or with other ingredients in a pilaf. For most cooked dishes the coarsely ground bulgar wheat is best, but use the finely ground grain for tabbouleh and kibbeh. For basic preparation, see pages 36 and 82.

CORIANDER This can be a spice or a herb. The green herb is sold fresh in bunches. It looks very much like flat-leaved parsley. It wilts quickly and should be kept in the refrigerator or with its stalks in water. The green leaves are never dried. The spice is a little round seed which is sold whole or ground. It cannot be used instead of the fresh leaves because they have a completely different taste.

COUSCOUS Hard wheat which has been coarsely ground, moistened and rolled in flour, is cooked by steaming. The couscous in this country is precooked and only needs soaking in three-quarters or more (see instructions on the packet) of its volume of water and heating through (usually with a little salt and a few tablespoons of butter or oil). The name couscous is also given to the whole dish – the grain and the garnish or stew.

DRIED LIMES Noumi Basra or Oman lemons are limes which have been dried until they are brown, sound hollow and have very dark brown insides. They have a delicious and unusual sour musty flavour and are sold whole or ground. You can make them yourself by leaving limes to dry out – for months – on a radiator. They are good in soups and stews. Put them in whole and pierce with a fork when they soften, or crack them open.

FILLO This is also spelt phylo (I have previously called it fila as we did in Egypt) and is paper-thin dough. The sheets are sold fresh and frozen in 300 g (10 oz) or 400 g (13 oz) airtight packets. They dry out quickly and must be taken out of the packet only when they are ready to be used.

HARISSA This is a fiery red pepper paste used in North Africa, particularly Tunisia, where people put it in everything and even spread it on bread.

MERGEZ Spicy North African sausages.

ORANGE-FLOWER WATER The distilled essence of the petals which is sold here is very diluted. It gives a delicate scent to all kinds of sweet dishes. You can put a few drops in cold or hot water to make a soothing drink.

POMEGRANATE SYRUP Boiled down juice of the sour (not sweet) fruit.

PRESERVED LEMONS OR LIMES Preserved in salt, these are a speciality of North Africa where they are used in all kinds of dishes. To make them, wash the lemons well and cut them, but not right through, in four (in two if limes) so they hold together at the stems. Sprinkle salt inside the slits: use 50 g (2 oz) for 500 g (1 lb) of lemons and press them down in a jar. When the juices run and the lemons begin to soften, press them down with a weight. Add extra lemon juice to cover and preserve them. They should be soft and mellow and ready to use within one month. Use one or two, chopped up (it is usual to remove the pulp and use only the peel).

ROSE-WATER The distilled essence of rose petals. The kind which is sold here is diluted. It is used to perfume desserts and pastries. A soothing bedtime drink is made by adding a few drops, with a tiny bit of sugar, to hot or cold water.

SUMAC A dark reddish-brown seed which has an unusual sharp flavour. It is used instead of lemon, either sprinkled on food in its ground form or infused in water and then strained.

TAHINA The oily paste of crushed sesame seeds.

TAMARIND The fibrous pod soaked in boiling water gives a wonderful sour juice. You can buy tamarind paste which is easier to use.

UTENSILS

When I travelled across Morocco I was told that the best way to cook was in unglazed earthenware pots over a charcoal fire, second best was in tinned copper on gas, and last was in aluminium. But every kitchen I went to, like the hardware stalls at the market, was full of enormous aluminium pots and pans.

You do not have to have special equipment, large heavy-based frying pans and saucepans (stainless steel is easiest to maintain), baking sheets and casseroles are all you require. You will need, too, a slotted spoon, a sieve or colander for washing rice, bulgar wheat and pulses, and a few special gadgets such as skewers for kebabs. But there is something very pleasing about using traditional equipment, so here are a few utensils you might look for on your travels.

A MOROCCAN TAGINE, called *tagine slaoui* because they are made in the town of Salé, is a shallow round earthenware pot with a high conical lid in which stews are simmered slowly and long. It can be put straight on top of the fire but there must always be a little water in it or it may crack. Egyptians have a deeper pot they call a *tagen.*

A COUSCOUSIÈRE (this is the French name) can be made in unglazed earthenware or in copper lined with tin. The usual aluminium ones are perfectly good. The lower part of the pot is to cook the stew in. The upper part, with a perforated bottom, holds the grain which is steamed in the aromatic vapours of the stew. This pot is not really necessary when you are using precooked couscous because the grain is ready very quickly – as soon as the steam comes through.

A **BRAZIER** or **BARBECUE**, and **SKEWERS**.

A PESTLE AND MORTAR. A food processor will do almost all the same tasks.

AN IRANIAN RICE PAN with a raffia lid covered by a removable cloth called a *damkoni.* A non-stick pan (to unmould the rice easily) with a cloth stretched underneath the lid to catch the steam is a perfect alternative. Electric Japanese rice pots, which are now popular with Iranians interested in ease and speed, can be used too.

A selection of ingredients and utensils

12

WHAT TO DRINK WITH MIDDLE EASTERN FOOD

Arak (or *raki*), the aniseed-flavoured aperitif distilled from grapes (in Morocco there is *mahia* made with figs and dates) is served with appetisers. Beer, too, and whisky are drunk with appetisers and with grilled foods. For those who will not have alcohol, the usual drinks, besides iced water, are chilled yogurt beaten with water or soda, or fresh fruit juice.

A Middle Eastern meal is greatly enhanced by wine (due to the prohibitions of Islam, local wines are for export rather than for the domestic market). The food needs simple robust wine with character and quality which can stand up to the amalgam of flavours, not great or complex wine.

Buy a dry fresh white and a robust and earthy red. Sweetness in foods will make a thin dry wine too acid and sour foods will turn it flat, but a young vigorous wine with rough fruit will go well with sour, sweet and savoury dishes. A fruity-flavoured wine will complement the fruit in a meat or chicken stew. When the dessert is fruit or a delicate pudding you can have a dessert wine, but no wine will be sweet enough for a pastry soaked in syrup, so serve Turkish coffee instead.

SERVING MIDDLE EASTERN FOOD Middle Eastern food customs are related to religious holidays and festivities, to the traditions of visiting and the obligations of hospitality, to shopping at the souk for seasonal ingredients and indeed to everything that is everyday life in that part of the world.

There are still traditional households where people sit on a divan or on cushions at low round tables – large metal trays on folding wooden legs – and eat with their hands (the three fingers of the right hand) from the serving plate. There are still receptions where a succession of dishes – roast lamb, pies, meat stews, poultry, grains, and different kinds of vegetables, puddings and pastries – follow one another, and where scented water is poured from a silver ewer into a basin for guests to wash their hands while incense burns in a little holder. And there are buffets where dozens of appetisers jostle for space on the table.

Village life still revolves around the rhythm of the seasons – the milling of the grain, the drying of vegetables and fruit and the making of preserves in preparation for winter. Pots may be sent to cook in the ashes at the public oven and meats roasted over charcoal.

The recipes collected in this book are from countries that have much in common, yet the manner of eating and serving them may be very different. So use the dishes as you would your own: in a three course meal, as snacks or for a buffet. They will represent a small but wonderful taste of a very large repertoire of cooking.

SOUPS

Soups are not usually part of a Middle Eastern menu but may be served alone as the meal itself with bread to dip in. On cold winter days heart-warming meaty soups, which are almost as rich as stews, are prepared with different vegetables, pulses and dried fruit.

Soups are also for special occasions and there are national soups and soups traditionally sold in the street. The Moroccan bean soup, Harira, is eaten throughout the 30 days of Ramadan.

The soups I have included can be served either as a first course or the more substantial ones will provide a whole meal in the Middle Eastern manner.

SHORBAT ADS

Lentil soup   Serves 6–8

2–3 tablespoons olive oil
2 medium-size onions, chopped coarsely
3 garlic cloves, crushed
500 g (1 lb) red lentils
1.75 litres (3 pints) meat or chicken stock
1 teaspoon ground cumin
1 teaspoon ground coriander
a pinch of chilli powder (optional)
juice of 1 lemon
salt
a small bunch of fresh parsley or dill, chopped finely, to garnish

This homely and nourishing Egyptian soup is very popular in our family, and easy to make for a large number of people.

Heat the oil in a large pan and cook the onions, stirring occasionally, until very brown. Stir in the garlic.

Add the lentils and stock and bring to the boil. Remove any scum. Stir in the cumin, coriander and chilli powder, if using, and simmer for 1 hour or until the lentils have disintegrated. Add salt when the lentils have begun to soften.

If necessary, add water to thin the soup to a light-cream consistency. Stir in the lemon juice and serve in warm bowls, garnishing each with a little parsley or dill.

Variations: Add 125 g (4 oz) rice or broken vermicelli 15 minutes before the end. Or add 2 tomatoes, skinned and chopped, when the soup is ready and just let them soften. Or add 500 g (1 lb) well rinsed and shredded spinach and cook for a further 10 minutes.

SHORBA BIL HOUT

Algerian fish soup

Serves 6

4 tablespoons olive oil

2 onions, chopped

6 garlic cloves, crushed

2 large potatoes, cubed

500 g (1 lb) tomatoes, skinned and diced

2 bay leaves

½ teaspoon dried thyme

¼ teaspoon saffron strands, crushed in a little water (optional)

1–2 teaspoons harissa, or 1½ teaspoons paprika and a pinch of chilli powder

2.25 litres (4 pints) water

1 kg (2 lb) cod or haddock fillets, skinned

juice of ½–1 lemon

2 eggs, beaten

salt and pepper

Any fish will do for this creamy spicy soup. If you use saffron it gives the soup a brilliant yellow colour and a delicious aroma.

Heat the oil in a large pan and fry the onions until soft. Add the garlic and let it just begin to colour.

Add the potatoes, tomatoes, bay leaves, thyme, saffron, if using, and salt and pepper and harissa (to taste) or paprika mixture. Cover with the water and simmer for 15 minutes or until the potatoes are soft.

Add the fish and cook for 7 minutes or until it begins to flake. Remove from the heat and take out the bay leaves. Purée the soup in a blender. Return it to the pan and add the lemon juice to taste. Check the seasonings and add more water if the soup is too thick.

Just before serving, heat the soup until simmering. Add a ladleful of soup to the eggs and mix well. Stir quickly into the soup. Turn off the heat at once so that the eggs thicken the soup but do not curdle it.

SHORBA BEIDA

Algerian egg and lemon soup

Serves 6

2–3 chicken breasts

1 large onion, chopped

125 g (4 oz) chick-peas, soaked for 1 hour and drained

2.25 litres (4 pints) water

½ teaspoon ground cinnamon

125 g (4 oz) vermicelli

This egg and lemon soup is enriched with chick-peas.

Put the chicken breasts in a large saucepan with the onion, chick-peas and water. Bring to the boil, remove any scum, and then add the cinnamon and pepper to taste. Simmer, covered, for 1 hour or until the chick-peas are soft. Take the chicken out of the soup and remove the skin and bones if you wish. Return to the soup and add salt to taste and the vermicelli and cook for 10 minutes longer. Add the parsley and turn off the heat.

a bunch of fresh parsley,
chopped finely

2 egg yolks

juice of 1 lemon

salt and pepper

Just before serving, heat the soup. Beat the egg yolks and lemon juice together in a large bowl, and then beat in 2 ladlefuls of soup. Pour this mixture back into the saucepan, stirring vigorously. Remove from the heat to avoid the yolks curdling.

ADS BI HAMUD

Lentil soup with spinach and lemon   Serves 6

375 g (12 oz) green lentils,
soaked for 1 hour

1 kg (2 lb) spinach, rinsed
well and chopped

4 tablespoons olive oil

2 onions, cut in half and
sliced thinly

5 garlic cloves, sliced

1 tablespoon plain flour

300 ml (½ pint) water

juice of 1½ lemons

salt and pepper

This is a Lebanese mountain soup.

Drain the lentils. Put them in a pan with enough water to cover and simmer for 30 minutes or until very tender. Season to taste with salt and pepper towards the end.

Add the spinach to the lentils.

Heat the oil in a frying pan and cook the onions until soft. Add the garlic and, when the aroma rises, add the flour and stir well. Gradually add the water to make a smooth sauce. Pour into the soup.

Add the lemon juice and more water, if necessary, and simmer until thick.

Serve very hot.

HARIRA

Moroccan soup   Serves 8

250 g (8 oz) chicken,
preferably from the leg,
diced

250 g (8 oz) chick-peas,
soaked for 1 hour and
drained

1 onion, chopped coarsely

250 g (8 oz) tomatoes,
skinned and chopped

2.75 litres (5 pints) chicken
stock

1 teaspoon ground
cinnamon

Moroccans break the daily fast on this nutritious soup during the month-long fast of Ramadan. Late at night the signal to eat is given – a thunder of cannon and a roll of drums. The soup is followed by music, and singing and dancing by the men. Two hours later the main meal begins and often continues until dawn.

At other times Harira is sold in the souks all day, the vendors put out tables and ladle the thick broth from huge cauldrons into ornately painted bowls.

Every family has its own special recipe for this much-loved soup.

125 g (4 oz) rice or vermicelli	Put the chicken, chick-peas, onion and tomatoes in a pan and pour over the stock.
a bunch of fresh coriander or parsley, chopped finely	Bring to the boil, remove any scum and add the cinammon and pepper to taste. Simmer for 1 hour or until the chick-peas are soft, adding
3 eggs, beaten	salt towards the end.
salt and pepper	Add the rice or vermicelli 15 minutes before serving. Finally add the coriander or parsley,
2 lemons, cut into wedges, to serve	take the soup off the heat and beat in the eggs vigorously – they will cook enough to thicken

the soup. (A flour and water paste may be used but I prefer to leave it out.) Serve hot with the lemon wedges.

DJARI BEL FOUL

Algerian bean soup   Serves 6

This soup can be made quite hot and peppery.

2 tablespoons olive oil	Heat the oil in a pan and fry the onion until golden. Add the beans and stock and cook for about 45 minutes or until the beans are tender.
1 onion, chopped	
250 g (8 oz) white beans, soaked for 1 hour	Season with salt and pepper, add the harissa or chilli powder, tomatoes and vermicelli and
2.25 litres (4 pints) meat or chicken stock	cook for another 10 minutes. Add the parsley and serve.
½ teaspoon harissa or a pinch of chilli powder	
3 large tomatoes, skinned and chopped	
125 g (4 oz) vermicelli	
a bunch of fresh parsley, chopped finely	
salt and pepper	

ASHE MAST

Green yogurt soup

Serves 6

1½ tablespoons olive oil

1 large onion, chopped

2 tablespoons red lentils

125 g (4 oz) long-grain or basmati rice

1 litre (1¾ pints) water

500 g (1 lb) spinach, rinsed well and shredded

a small bunch of fresh coriander, chopped

a small bunch of fresh chives, chopped finely

a small bunch of fresh parsley, chopped

600 ml (1 pint) natural yogurt

salt and pepper

To garnish:

1 large onion, sliced

1½ tablespoons olive oil

2 teaspoons dried mint

This lovely fresh-tasting cold soup is Iranian. It is ideal for a summer day.

Heat the oil and cook the chopped onion until it is soft. Add salt and pepper to taste, the lentils and rice. Cover with the water, bring to the boil and simmer for 20 minutes or until the lentils and rice are tender.

Add the spinach, coriander, chives and parsley, and cook for 10 minutes or until the

Harira (Moroccan soup)

Djari Bel Foul (Algerian bean soup)

spinach is soft. Add a little more water if the soup is too thick. Let it cool.

Beat the yogurt, stir it in and pour the soup into a serving bowl.

For the garnish, cook the sliced onion in the oil until golden. Add the mint and cook, stirring, for a minute longer. Spoon the mixture over the soup.

Variations: To serve the soup hot: beat the yogurt in and heat it through without letting it boil so that it does not curdle. I sometimes also add the juice of 1 lemon. Or use split peas instead of lentils: boil them for 20 minutes before the rice is put in.

Ashe Mast (Green yogurt soup)

APPETISERS, VEGETABLES AND SIDE DISHES

Appetisers are for entertaining and every day. It is usual to have a large assortment at parties, from simple ones like olives, pickles and nuts, to pies, salads and purées. They are presented on individual serving plates around the room or placed on a coffee table for guests to pick at. Their sharpness and spiciness are meant to whet the appetite, but by the time the usually-late dinner arrives most people have eaten enough. At a family meal the dishes are put on the table and the appetisers become side dishes.

I have given many recipes in this chapter because they are so versatile. You can serve several appetisers – with a variety of flavours, textures and colours – for people to have a little taste of each, or you can choose one alone as a first course.

There are salads and cold vegetables, which you can offer with meat and fish, and there are egg dishes and pies which make light meals in themselves accompanied by yogurt and a fresh salad. The list could contain meatballs and fish fritters, but I have given more vegetable *mezze* because vegetables are one of the most important, and to me, the most attractive features of Middle Eastern cooking.

Stuffed vegetables and vegetables cooked in oil are also served as a separate course – often to start the meal, sometimes as the third course, after meat – but I have put them all in this chapter.

PATLICAN TAVA

Fried aubergine slices   Serves 8–10

4 medium-size aubergines

oil for frying

salt

For the tomato topping:

1 tablespoon olive oil

1 garlic clove, crushed

3 large tomatoes, skinned
and chopped

1 tablespoon wine vinegar

2 teaspoons sugar

1 tablespoon currants
(optional)

1 tablespoon pine kernels,
toasted (optional)

a small bunch of fresh
parsley, chopped finely

salt and pepper

For the yogurt topping:

300 ml (½ pint) sheep's
milk yogurt or strained
yogurt

1 garlic clove, crushed
(optional)

*Two of the simplest and most wonderful ways of
serving aubergines are Turkish. Slices cut lengthways
are fried in hot oil, topped with thick yogurt or with
fresh tomato sauce, and served cold.*

*For every day, do one or the other. But for a party
it makes an attractive presentation to do both. Slice
the aubergines into smaller rounds and alternate the
two toppings as in a chess board.*

Cut the aubergines lengthways, or in rounds, in
5 mm (¼-inch) thick slices. Sprinkle with salt
and leave for 30 minutes for the juices to run.
Rinse and pat dry with kitchen paper.

Heat the oil in a large pan until hot and fry
the slices very quickly, turning once, until soft
when you prick them with a fork. Drain on
kitchen paper and arrange on a flat serving
dish.

To make the tomato sauce, heat the oil in a
pan and cook the garlic. Add the tomatoes,
vinegar, sugar, salt and pepper to taste and
currants, if using, and cook for 2–3 minutes.
Spread a little of the sauce on half the
aubergine slices and sprinkle with the pine
kernels, if using, and parsley.

Flavour the yogurt with garlic, if using, and
spread over the remaining aubergine. Serve
cold.

Variation: For those who do not like frying,
simmer the aubergine slices in a mixture of
tomato juice and water for 20 minutes or until
tender. Drain. The addition of 2 garlic cloves,
sliced, 1 tablespoon of dried mint, 1 tablespoon
of vinegar and 2 teaspoons of sugar will
improve the flavour. Finish as above.

SALATET FELFEL

Roast peppers in olive oil   Serves 6

6 green, red and yellow peppers
4 tablespoons olive oil
salt and pepper
To garnish:
a handful of black olives
2 slices of feta cheese, cubed (optional)

When peppers are roasted their flesh becomes deliciously soft and their flavour changes, too. But they must be fleshy ones or it is not worth the trouble of peeling them.

This dish is usually made with green peppers, but it is more attractive with yellow and red ones added.

Preheat the oven to Gas Mark 9/240°C/475°F.

Put the peppers in the oven for about 30 minutes or until they are brown all over, turning them over once.

Put the peppers into a polythene bag, close tightly and leave for about 10 minutes – this makes peeling easier.

Peel the peppers, pull off the stems, cut them open and remove the seeds, keeping the juices. Cut the flesh into largish strips or squares and dress with their juices, the oil, and salt and pepper to taste.

Garnish with the olives and pieces of cheese, if using.

Variation: For a stronger flavour, add 1 tablespoon or more of wine vinegar, 2 garlic cloves, crushed, and a good pinch of chilli powder to the dressing.

Yaprak Dolmasi (Stuffed vine leaves)

Patlican Tava (Fried aubergine slices)

Salatet Felfel (Roast peppers in olive oil)

YAPRAK DOLMASI

Stuffed vine leaves   Serves 6

250 g (8 oz) fresh or 227 g
(8 oz) packet of preserved
vine leaves

125 ml (4 fl oz) olive oil

juice of 1 lemon

1 teaspoon sugar

salt and pepper

For the filling:

5 tablespoons olive oil

500 g (1 lb) onions,
chopped

25 g (1 oz) pine kernels

250 g (8 oz) long-grain
rice, washed and drained

25 g (1 oz) currants

1 tablespoon sugar

300 ml (½ pint) water

a small bunch of fresh mint,
chopped finely

a small bunch of fresh dill,
chopped finely

a small bunch of fresh
parsley, chopped finely

salt and pepper

*You can find stuffed vine leaves in every Middle
Eastern country. They are eaten hot or cold, and the
many different fillings combine rice with meat (those
with meat are eaten hot), onions, tomatoes and all
kinds of nuts, dried fruit, herbs and spices. There is
one – a Lenten dish from Syria – which has a filling
of bulgar wheat and split peas. They are sometimes
served with a tomato or an egg and lemon sauce, and
can also be popped into a stew. In the Arab world the
rice is used raw; in Turkey it is cooked first.*

*This recipe, a classic one from Turkey, is to be
served cold as an appetiser.*

Blanch fresh vine leaves for a few seconds in
boiling water until limp. Soak leaves preserved
in brine in boiling water and then in 2 changes
of cold water for 1 hour to remove the salt.

To make the filling, heat the oil in a pan and
fry the onions until golden. Add the pine
kernels and let them brown lightly. Add the
rice and stir until transparent. Add the currants,
sugar and water and salt and pepper to taste.
Stir well and cook, covered, for 15 minutes.
Stir in the herbs.

Line the bottom of a heavy-based pan with
torn discarded vine leaves (or lettuce leaves) to
prevent the stuffed ones from sticking and
burning.

To fill the vine leaves, lay a leaf on a plate,
vein-side up. Put 1 tablespoon of filling in a
line along the stem edge. Fold this edge over it,
then fold both sides in towards the centre and
roll up like a small cigar. Fill the rest in the
same way.

Pack the leaves tightly in layers in the pan.
Mix together the olive oil, lemon juice and
sugar and season with salt and pepper. Pour
over the leaves, adding enough water to just
cover them. Place a plate on top to hold the
leaves down, cover and cook for about 1 hour.

Let them cool in the pan before turning out.

SALATA BALADI

Mixed salad Arab-style (Pictured on page 5) Serves 6

*1 small cos lettuce or ½
small white cabbage,
shredded*

3 firm tomatoes, diced

*1 green pepper, de-seeded
and diced (optional)*

½ cucumber, diced

*5 spring onions or 1 small
onion, chopped*

*16 radishes, sliced
(optional)*

*a bunch of fresh parsley or
coriander, chopped coarsely*

*a few sprigs of fresh mint,
chopped (optional)*

For the dressing:

4 tablespoons olive oil

juice of 1 lemon, or more

salt and pepper

This popular salad can be served with everything.

Mix together the lettuce or cabbage, tomatoes,
green pepper, if using, cucumber, onion,
radishes, if using, parsley or coriander and
mint, if using.

To make the dressing, beat together the oil
and lemon juice and season to taste. Just before
serving the salad, pour over the dressing and
mix well.

Variations: To make it into *Fattoush*, toast an
opened-out pitta bread, break it into small
pieces and sprinkle over the salad. Or add a
sprinkling of sumac and a handful of
pomegranate seeds.

BABA GHANOUSH

Aubergine and tahina salad Serves 4

1 large aubergine

juice of 2 lemons

3 tablespoons tahina

2 garlic cloves, crushed

salt

*a few sprigs of fresh
parsley, chopped finely, to
garnish*

*This delicious purée is as popular as hummus and they
are often served together. Prepare warm pitta bread to
dip in it.*

Roast the aubergine under a grill, turning it a
few times, until the skin is black and blistered
and the flesh feels very soft when you press it.
Peel the aubergine and squeeze out the juice.
Put it in a blender or food processor with the
lemon juice, tahina, garlic, salt to taste and 2
tablespoons of water and purée until smooth.

Spread the cream on a flat plate and sprinkle
with the parsley.

HUMMUS BI TAHINA

Chick-pea dip

175 g (6 oz) chick-peas, soaked for at least 1 hour

4 tablespoons tahina

juice of 2 lemons, or to taste

4 garlic cloves, crushed (optional)

salt

2 tablespoons olive oil, to serve

Serve this well-known Arab cream salad with warm pitta bread. Accompany with a plate of radishes, spring onions and pickled cucumbers or turnips.

Drain the chick-peas, place in a pan with fresh water to cover and cook for 1 hour or until soft.

Purée the chick-peas in a blender with enough of their cooking water to make a thick paste. Tasting frequently, add the tahina, lemon juice, garlic, if using, and a little salt and blend very thoroughly to a light cream (you may need a little more water). Spread the cream flat on a plate and sprinkle with the olive oil.

Variation: Add 1 teaspoon of ground cumin to the cream and garnish with a sprinkling of paprika and cumin.

TARAMASALATA

Smoked cod's roe dip

125 g (4 oz) piece of smoked cod's roe

juice of 1 lemon, or more to taste

125 g (4 oz) cream cheese

½ small onion, grated (optional)

This light and easy version of the famous smoked cod's roe cream has been adopted by a few Greek restaurants in Britain. Make it as an appetiser to dip into with pitta bread.

Wash the cod's roe, put it in the food processor (leave the skin on as it gives a stronger colour) with the lemon juice and blend to a smooth paste, adding more lemon juice if necessary.

Add the cream cheese and blend for only a very short time so that it does not become too soft (it can become almost liquid).

Stir in the onion, if using, and serve with pitta bread cut into triangles.

Baba Ghanoush (Aubergine and tahina salad)
Hummus Bi Tahina (Chick-pea dip)
Taramasalata (Smoked cod's roe dip)

Moroccan chicken pie

Serves 8

6 tablespoons olive oil

8 chicken drumsticks

1 kg (2 lb) onions, grated or chopped finely

2 teaspoons ground cinnamon

a good pinch of saffron strands, crushed in a little water (optional)

500 g (1 lb) puff pastry

flour for rolling

butter for greasing

1 egg, separated

125 g (4 oz) flaked almonds, toasted

salt and pepper

The traditional pastry for this pie is a yeast dough kneaded for half an hour to great elasticity, rolled into balls, anointed with oil, then pulled into paper-thin sheets. Here is a simpler version using bought puff pastry. It makes a delicious pie.

Heat the oil in a large pan and cook the drumsticks and onions over a very low heat. Add 1½ teaspoons of the cinnamon and the saffron, if using, and season with salt and pepper. Cook gently, stirring occasionally, for 30 minutes or until the chicken is so tender that it comes off the bone.

Lift out the drumsticks, remove and discard the skin and bones and cut the flesh into small pieces.

Preheat the oven to Gas Mark 6/200°C/ 400°F.

Continue to cook the onions, stirring often, until all the liquid has gone and they have turned into a soft golden cream. Return the chicken to the pan and take off the heat.

Divide the pastry into two balls. Roll out the first one, thinly, on a floured surface with a floured rolling pin. Lift it up and ease it into a greased 28 cm (11-inch) round ovenproof dish or tray, letting the pastry hang a little over the sides. Trim the edges with a knife, prick with a fork in several places, and bake blind for 15 minutes (it does not matter if it puffs up). Brush with the egg white and put it back in the oven for 5 minutes. This will prevent the pastry from becoming soggy with the filling.

Spread the filling inside the pastry shell and sprinkle with the almonds.

Roll out the second ball of pastry, as before, and place it on top, sealing the edges well. Brush with the egg yolk and bake in the oven for 30 minutes, or until crisp and brown.

Serve hot, sprinkled with the remaining cinnamon.

BOREK

Little fillo savouries (Pictured on page 5)   Makes about 60

500 g (1 lb) fillo pastry

175 g (6 oz) butter, melted

For the cheese filling:

375 g (12 oz) feta cheese,
mashed, or farmhouse
Cheddar, grated

2 eggs

2 teaspoons dried mint

pepper

For the spinach filling:

1 kg (2 lb) fresh spinach,
rinsed well, or 500 g (1 lb)
frozen whole-leaf spinach,
thawed

125 g (4 oz) feta cheese,
mashed, or cottage cheese,
drained well

a good pinch of ground
nutmeg

2 eggs

salt and pepper

1

You can find these savouries in most countries of the
Middle East, often with their Turkish name borek.
They come in different shapes and with a variety of
fillings. There are also different ways of making the
paper-thin dough, but now that fillo is readily
available you cannot do better than to use it.

As the two most popular fillings are spinach and
cheese, and the most common shapes are fingers and
triangles, I have given the recipe for these.

To make the cheese filling, mix the cheese,
eggs and mint together in a bowl. Season with
pepper.
    For the spinach filling, cook the fresh leaves
in a covered pan over a low heat until they
crumple. Drain well (it is usual, but not
necessary, to chop the leaves coarsely). Or
squeeze the water out of the frozen spinach.
Place the spinach in a bowl and stir in the
cheese, nutmeg and eggs and season with a
little pepper and salt, if necessary. (Feta has
quite a strong flavour and is quite salty.)
    Preheat the oven to Gas Mark 4/180°C/
350°F. Butter two large baking sheets. Cut the
sheets of filo into rectangular strips about 8 cm
(3 inches) wide – this will make rather small
pastries, but in the Middle East and for
entertaining 'small is beautiful'. Put the strips
in a pile so that they do not dry out too
quickly.
    To make cheese fingers, brush the top strip
very lightly with melted butter. Put 1 heaped
teaspoon of cheese filling at one end and roll
up like a swiss roll. Turn the ends in about a
third of the way to trap the filling, then
continue to roll with the sides seemingly open
(1). Repeat with more strips until all the filling
has gone. Then place side by side on one of the
baking sheets and brush the tops very lightly
with butter.
    To make spinach triangles, brush a strip of

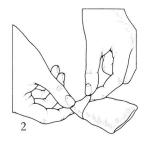

fillo with melted butter, put 1 heaped teaspoon of filling at one end about 2 cm (¾ inch) from the edge and fold one corner up over it. Then fold again and again (2) until the whole strip is folded into a small triangle (make sure you close any holes, as liquid from the filling can ooze out). Repeat until all the filling and strips have gone. Place close to each other on the remaining baking sheet and brush the tops lightly with melted butter.

Bake the cheese fingers and spinach triangles for 30 minutes or until crisp and golden. Serve hot.

BRIOUAT BEL KEFTA

Moroccan meat pies   Makes 8

| |
3 tablespoons olive oil

2 onions, chopped

500 g (1 lb) minced lamb or beef

3 teaspoons ground cinnamon

a pinch of chilli powder (optional)

a bunch of fresh parsley, chopped finely

a bunch of fresh coriander, chopped finely

6 eggs, beaten

500 g (1 lb) puff pastry

flour for rolling

oil for deep-frying

salt and pepper

Briouat Bel Kefta (Moroccan meat pies), in preparation

In Morocco, pastry is made by dabbing a tray, placed upside down over a fire, with a very soft dough until a round sheet as thin as paper is formed. Bought puff pastry rolled very thin makes a quick and respectable alternative. The spicy filling is delicious. You can make it very hot with chilli powder.

Heat the oil in a pan and fry the onions until golden. Add the meat, half the cinnamon and the chilli powder, if using, season with salt and pepper and fry, stirring occasionally, until the meat mixture is dry. Add the parsley and coriander and stir in the eggs. Keep stirring and cook for a minute or so until the eggs set.

Cut the pastry into 8 pieces. Make little balls and roll out, on a floured surface with a floured rolling pin, as thinly as possible. Place 2 heaped tablespoons of filling on one side near the centre of each pastry round (1) and fold the pastry over the filling. Pinch the edges together to close the little pies firmly (2).

Heat the oil for deep-frying until fairly hot and fry the pies until well browned, turning over once. Drain on kitchen paper. Serve very hot, sprinkled with the remaining cinnamon.

Variation: Do not fry the pies. Place them on a greased baking sheet, brush the tops with egg

and bake in an oven preheated to Gas Mark 5/
190°C/375°F for 30 minutes or until brown.
Serve hot, sprinkled with the remaining
cinnamon.

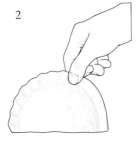

BIBER DOLMASI

Stuffed peppers   Serves 6

6 large or 12 small peppers

150 ml (¼ pint) olive oil

*2 large spanish onions,
chopped finely*

2 tablespoons pine kernels

*250 g (8 oz) pudding rice,
washed and drained*

2 tablespoons currants

1 tablespoon sugar

500 ml (1 pint) water

*a bunch of mixed fresh
parsley, mint and dill,
chopped finely*

tomato slices (optional)

salt and pepper

*This Turkish dish is served cold. It is usually made
with smallish green peppers, but you can use larger
ones and different colours to make a pleasing contrast.*

Cut a small slice from the stem end of each
pepper and remove the core and seeds.
Preheat the oven to Gas Mark 5/190°C/
375°F.
Heat 5 tablespoons of the oil in a saucepan
and fry the onions until golden. Add the pine
kernels and, when they begin to colour, add
the rice and cook, stirring, until translucent.
Add the currants, sugar, and three-quarters of
the water and season with salt and pepper.
Cook, covered, for 15 minutes, and then stir in
the herbs.
Pack the filling into the peppers and cover
with the tops or, if you prefer, follow the
Turkish custom and cover with slices of
tomato. Place in a baking dish, open-side up,
and pour in the remaining oil and water. Cover
with a lid or foil and bake for 40 minutes.
Uncover and bake for a further 20 minutes

until the peppers are soft. Leave to cool.

Variation: Use this filling for other vegetables, such as aubergines, tomatoes or courgettes, and serve cold.

TERBIYELI DOLMASI

Sweet and sour chard or spinach beet leaves   Serves 6

500 (1 lb) chard or spinach beet leaves, rinsed well

600 ml (1 pint) water

For the filling:

4 tablespoons vegetable oil

1 large onion, chopped coarsely

500 g (1 lb) risotto rice, washed and drained

1 tablespoon dried mint

juice of ½ lemon

1.2 litres (2 pints) water

salt

For the sauce:

4 eggs

juice of 2 lemons

1–2 tablespoons sugar

salt and pepper

In Turkey, large chard or spinach beet leaves are used like vine leaves and filled with rice. In this dish, their delicate flavour is enhanced by a sweet and sour egg and lemon sauce. You can use large spinach leaves in the same way.

To make the filling, heat the oil in a pan and fry the onion until soft. Add the rice, mint and lemon juice and season with salt. Pour in the water, stir well and cook, covered, for 15 minutes or until the water has been absorbed and the rice is tender. Cool.

Meanwhile, cut off the chard or beet stems but do not throw them away. Bring a large pan of water to the boil and plunge in the chard or spinach beet leaves for about 1 minute or until limp. Do not overcook. Drain immediately. Line the bottom of a pan with the stems.

Open out each leaf carefully and lay it flat, vein-side up. Place 1 tablespoon of the filling at one end (preferably not the stem end) and roll up, folding the two sides in towards the centre when you are midway.

Pack the rolls tightly in layers on top of the stems (these will protect them from burning). Pour the water over them, lay a plate on top and cook very gently for about 30 minutes. Turn out on a serving plate and reserve the cooking liquid.

To make the sauce, beat the eggs and lemon juice with about 150 ml (¼ pint) of the cooking liquid and pour into a small saucepan. Add sugar, salt and pepper to taste and stir constantly over a low heat until the sauce thickens. Do not let the sauce boil. Pour it over the stuffed leaves and serve cold.

TABBOULEH

Parsley and bulgar wheat salad   Serves 6–8

125 g (4 oz) medium-fine bulgar wheat

juice of 2 lemons, or more

5 tablespoons olive oil

6 spring onions or 1 small onion, chopped finely

300 g (10 oz) flat-leaved parsley, chopped finely

75 g (3 oz) fresh mint, chopped finely, or 2 tablespoons dried mint

3 tomatoes, skinned and diced

salt and pepper

cos lettuce leaves (from the heart), to serve

The most popular – even supreme – Arab salad is a village dish of Syria and the Lebanon which became an institution when it was adopted by cafés as an appetiser to accompany the local spirit, arak. Sixty years ago it was made with a large proportion of wheat, these days it is nearly all green and sharp with lemon juice. Serve it as an appetiser, as a first course, or to accompany grilled foods. The herbs are best chopped either by hand or in a food processor just before serving.

Taratorlu Kereviz (Celeriac and carrot tarator)

Tabbouleh (Parsley and bulgar wheat salad)

An hour before you are ready to serve, soak the bulgar wheat in cold water for about 15 minutes. Rinse and squeeze out the excess water. Dress with the lemon juice and salt and pepper to taste. Leave until it is plump and tender. Stir in the oil.

Mix together the spring onions or onion, bulgar wheat and herbs. Taste and adjust the seasoning and add more lemon juice if necessary. Transfer to a large flat serving dish and sprinkle the tomatoes over the top. Dig the lettuce leaf scoops in around the edges or serve them in a separate bowl.

Slata Michwiya
(Tunisian grilled salad)

SLATA MICHWIYA

Tunisian grilled salad   Serves 6

3 small onions

4 green and/or red and
yellow peppers

2 large tomatoes

1 chilli, chopped

juice of 1 lemon

3–4 tablespoons olive oil

1 tablespoon capers

2 eggs, hard-boiled and cut
in wedges lengthways

100 g (3½ oz) can of tuna,
drained

salt

*All the vegetables acquire a delicious mellow flavour
when they are roasted. I also like to make this salad
without the last three ingredients.*

Preheat the oven to Gas Mark 9/240°C/475°F.

Although the vegetables are usually cooked
under the grill it is easier to roast them in the
oven. Put the onions and peppers in and cook
them for 30 minutes or until the skins are very
brown and they feel soft. Put the tomatoes in
for 4 minutes.

Put the roasted peppers straight into a
polythene bag, close it tightly and leave them
for about 10 minutes. This makes them easier
to peel.

Peel, de-seed if necessary, and cut the
vegetables into small pieces and place in a
bowl. Stir in the chilli, lemon juice, oil and
capers and season with salt. Arrange on a
shallow serving dish with the eggs and crumble
the tuna on top.

TARATORLU KEREVIZ

Celeriac and carrot tarator   Serves 4–6

1 large celeriac, cut into
matchsticks

3 large carrots, cut into
matchsticks

salt

For the sauce:

125 g (4 oz) hazelnuts,
ground coarsely

2 garlic cloves, crushed

4 tablespoons olive oil

3 tablespoons wine vinegar

*In Turkey all sorts of boiled vegetables, including
cauliflower and beans, are dressed with a nut sauce
called* tarator. *In this recipe, celeriac and carrots
make a good combination of flavour and colour and
yogurt is a refreshing addition to the sauce.*

Cook the celeriac and carrots in boiling salted
water briefly until they are both just tender.
Drain.

To make the sauce, place the ground nuts,
crushed garlic, oil, vinegar and yogurt in a food
processor and blend together. Season with the
chilli powder, if using, and add salt to taste.

Place the vegetables in a serving dish and

150 ml (¼ pint) natural
yogurt

a pinch of chilli powder
(optional)

salt

To garnish:

a sprig of fresh parsley,
chopped finely

½ teaspoon paprika

pour over the sauce. Garnish with the parsley
and paprika.

SLATIT QURA'A

Mashed courgette and tomato salad   Serves 6

4 tablespoons olive oil

2 large onions, chopped

2 garlic cloves, crushed

1 teaspoon ground cumin

500 g (1 lb) courgettes,
sliced thickly

2 tablespoons wine vinegar

a good pinch of chilli
powder (optional)

500 g (1 lb) tomatoes,
skinned and chopped

salt and pepper

This is a strongly flavoured North African appetiser.

Heat the oil in a large pan and fry the onions
until golden. Add the garlic and cumin and stir.
Add the courgettes, vinegar, salt and pepper to
taste, chilli powder, if used, and tomatoes.
Cover the pan and steam over a low heat for
10 minutes or until the courgettes are very
tender.

Mash the mixture with a fork or a potato
masher. Serve cold.

CELERIAC SALAD

Serves 4

2 celeriac, weighing about
1 kg (2 lb), chopped

3 garlic cloves, crushed

5 tablespoons olive oil

¼ teaspoon turmeric

2 teaspoons sugar

juice of 1 lemon

salt and pepper

*Turmeric gives this salad a hint of yellow and a
distinctive flavour.*

Put the celeriac in a saucepan with the rest of
the ingredients and enough water to cover.
Cook, uncovered, for 10–20 minutes or until
soft and the liquid is reduced. Serve cold.

Variation: Make this salad with other root
vegetables, such as potatoes, turnips or swedes.

EGGAH BEL SABANEH

Spinach omelette

Serves 4

| 2 tablespoons olive oil |
| 1 medium-size onion, chopped |
| 500 g (1 lb) spinach, rinsed well |
| a pinch of grated nutmeg |
| 2 tomatoes, skinned and cut into pieces |
| 50 g (2 oz) chick-peas, soaked and cooked (optional) |
| 4 large eggs (size 1–2), beaten |
| salt and pepper |

Almost every kind of vegetable is cooked with eggs, and spinach is especially popular. Many families have this kind of omelette in the refrigerator ready for an impromptu snack, or a packed lunch for children at school, or husbands at work. This is an Egyptian version.

Mahshi Tamatem (Stuffed tomatoes)

Eggah Bel Sabaneh (Spinach omelette)

Shakshouka (Vegetables with eggs)

Heat the oil in a large frying pan and cook the onion until golden. Squeeze the water out of the spinach leaves with your hands. Shred or leave them whole and add to the pan.

Stir in the nutmeg and tomatoes and salt and pepper to taste and cook until the spinach crumples. Add the chick-peas if you want a more substantial dish.

Pour in the eggs and mix gently. Cook, covered, over a very low heat for 10–15 minutes or until set. Put under a medium-hot grill to dry the top.

Turn out onto a serving plate and serve hot or cold, cut like a cake.

SHAKSHOUKA

Vegetables with eggs | Serves 4

4 tablespoons olive oil

1 onion, sliced

2 green peppers, de-seeded
and cut into strips

4 tomatoes, sliced

pepper or a pinch of chilli
powder (optional)

1 tablespoon chopped fresh
mint

4 large eggs (size 1–2)

salt

*This Tunisian dish, which has become popular in
most countries of the Middle East, can be varied by
adding spicy sausages, such as chorizos, or courgettes,
aubergines and potatoes.*

Heat the oil in a pan and fry the onion and
peppers until they are soft and the onions are
golden.

Add the tomatoes, sprinkle with a little salt
and pepper or chilli powder, if using, and the
mint. Break the eggs on top. Cook gently until
the eggs have set. Serve with bread.

MAHSHI TAMATEM

Stuffed tomatoes | Serves 4

4 extra large tomatoes

2 tablespoons olive oil

1 onion, chopped

250 g (8 oz) minced beef

1 tablespoon currants

2 tablespoons coarsely
chopped walnuts

½–1 teaspoon ground
cinnamon

½ teaspoon ground allspice

a small bunch of fresh
parsley, chopped finely

salt and pepper

Serve as a starter or a light main course.

Preheat the oven to Gas Mark 4/180°C/350°F.

Cut a slice off the top of the tomatoes, and
scoop out the seeds and some of the pulp.

Heat the oil in a pan and fry the onion until
golden. Add the beef and stir well until
browned all over. Stir in the currants, walnuts,
cinnamon to taste, allspice and parsley and
season with salt and pepper. Cook for 8
minutes.

Fill the tomatoes with the beef mixture and
cover with the tops. Put the tomatoes close
together in a small baking dish with a little
water over the bottom. Bake for 30 minutes or
until the tomatoes are soft, but not so soft that
they fall apart. Serve hot.

CACIK

Yogurt and cucumber salad

Serves 6

600 ml (1 pint) sheep's milk yogurt or strained yogurt
1–2 garlic cloves, crushed
a few sprigs of fresh mint or dill, chopped finely, or 1 tablespoon dried mint
1 large cucumber, peeled and chopped
2 tablespoons olive oil
salt and pepper

You will find this famous Turkish salad everywhere in the Middle East.

Season the yogurt with a little salt and pepper. Stir in the garlic and some of the mint or dill.

Just before you are ready to serve, mix in the cucumber. Garnish with a dribble of olive oil and a sprinkling of the remaining herb(s).

MAACOUDA BEL BATATA

Potato omelette

Serves 6

500 g (1 lb) potatoes, cut into pieces
2 large onions, chopped
3 tablespoons olive oil
2 garlic cloves, crushed
6 eggs
a bunch of fresh parsley, chopped finely
1½ teaspoons harissa, or 1 teaspoon paprika and a good pinch of chilli powder
salt
1 lemon, cut into wedges, to serve (optional)

This simple but substantial North African omelette makes a good snack meal accompanied by salad. It can be eaten hot or cold, and is an ideal food to take on a picnic.

Cook the potatoes in salted water until soft. Drain and mash with a fork.

Fry the onions in 2 tablespoons of the oil until soft and lightly coloured. Add the garlic and, when the aroma rises, stir the mixture into the potatoes. Beat in the eggs, one at a time, and add the parsley and harissa or paprika and chilli powder.

Heat the remaining oil in a large frying pan, pour in the egg and potato mixture, and cook over a very low heat for 10–15 minutes until the bottom sets. Place the pan under a hot grill for a few minutes until the top is firm and lightly browned.

Serve the omelette hot or cold, accompanied, if you like, by the lemon wedges.

SHLADA L'FILFIL

Cucumber relish   Serves 6

1 large cucumber, chopped
finely

½ spanish onion, chopped
finely

2 chillies, chopped finely

3 tablespoons olive oil

2 tablespoons wine vinegar

2 large tomatoes, skinned
and chopped

salt

*I call this refreshing salad a relish because it is
peppery and the ingredients are chopped small. There
is a strong Spanish influence on the cooking of
Tetouan in Morocco where it comes from. Chop the
tomatoes by hand and the rest in a food processor,
being careful not to turn everything into a mush.*

Mix the cucumber, onion and chillies in a
colander and sprinkle with salt. Leave to drain
for 30 minutes. Rinse if necessary.

Mix together the olive oil and vinegar and
pour over the cucumber mixture. Stir in the
tomatoes. Serve with bread or as an
accompaniment to grilled foods.

OMI HOURIYA

Mashed carrot salad (Pictured on page 5)   Serves 4

750 g (1½ lb) carrots

4 tablespoons olive oil

3 tablespoons wine vinegar

2 garlic cloves, crushed

1 teaspoon paprika

a good pinch of chilli
powder

2 teaspoons ground cumin

salt and pepper

a few black olives, to
garnish

*This is a Tunisian salad to eat with bread. It is hot
and spicy to whet the appetite. If you have some
harissa use it instead of the paprika and chilli powder.*

Boil the carrots in salted water until soft. Drain
thoroughly.

Mash the carrots with a fork or chop them
finely. Add the oil, vinegar, garlic and spices
and season to taste.

Serve cold, garnished with the olives.

NAZKHATOUN

Aubergine salad
Serves 6

2 aubergines

2 garlic cloves, crushed

a few sprigs of fresh mint, chopped finely, or 2 teaspoons dried mint

2 tablespoons olive oil

2 tablespoons sour pomegranate syrup or juice of 1 lemon

3 tomatoes, skinned and chopped

salt and pepper

This salad is from Iran.

Place the aubergines under a grill and cook until the skins are black and blistered and the flesh feels soft inside. Put them in a colander and peel them as soon as they are cool enough to handle; then squeeze out the juice.

Chop or mash the aubergines or purée them in a food processor. Add the garlic, mint, oil and syrup or juice, season to taste with salt and pepper and mix well. Fold in the tomatoes gently and serve cold.

FASULYA PILAKISI

Beans in oil (Pictured on page 4)
Serves 6

250 g (8 oz) white beans, soaked for at least 1 hour

1 large onion, chopped

150 ml (¼ pint) olive oil

2 garlic cloves, sliced

2 celery sticks with leaves, diced

1 carrot, diced

2 tomatoes, skinned and diced

2 teaspoons sugar

salt

This white bean salad is the most common appetiser in Turkey.

Drain the beans, boil in fresh water for 10 minutes, and then simmer for about 30 minutes.

Cook the onion in the oil until soft, add the garlic and brown slightly. Add the celery, carrot, tomatoes, sugar and salt to taste. Stir in the drained beans and enough water to cover. Cook, covered, for about 1 hour. Serve cold.

BORANI ESFENAJ

Spinach and yogurt salad   Serves 4

500 g (1 lb) spinach, rinsed well

1 onion, chopped

2 tablespoons olive oil

2 garlic cloves, crushed

300 ml (½ pint) natural yogurt

salt and pepper

A delicate and fresh Iranian salad.

Drain the spinach and squeeze out all the water with your hands.

Fry the onion in the oil until golden. Add the garlic and when it begins to colour, add the spinach and salt and pepper to taste. Cook gently, turning the spinach over until it crumples into a soft mass. Let it cool.

Mix with the yogurt in a bowl and chill before serving.

TUNISIAN CAULIFLOWER FRITTERS

                                                            Serves 6

1 large cauliflower, cut into florets

75 g (3 oz) plain flour

2 eggs

juice of 1 lemon

125 g (4 oz) Gruyère or farmhouse Cheddar, grated

¼ teaspoon ground nutmeg

a good pinch of chilli powder (optional)

1 garlic clove, crushed (optional)

oil for deep-frying

salt

Boil the cauliflower in lightly salted water for 5 minutes until just tender. Drain and chop finely.

Beat the flour with the eggs and lemon juice until well blended. Add the cheese and nutmeg – and, if using, the chilli powder and garlic – and stir in the cauliflower. Leave for 30 minutes.

Heat the oil for deep-frying until hot, but not smoking. Carefully drop in tablespoons of the mixture and fry until browned, turning once. Drain on kitchen paper and serve hot.

GREEN VEGETABLES

3 tablespoons olive oil

1 onion, chopped

2 garlic cloves, crushed

250 g (8 oz) broad beans

2 artichoke hearts, cut in 4 (optional)

juice of 1 lemon

1 teaspoon sugar

500 g (1 lb) spinach or chard, rinsed well

salt and pepper

This summer dish of cooked green vegetables, found in Turkey and elsewhere, is as good cold as it is hot.

Heat the oil in a pan and fry the onion until golden. Add the garlic and, when it begins to colour, add the broad beans and artichoke hearts, if using. Cover with water, add the lemon juice and sugar, and season with salt and pepper. Simmer until the vegetables are only just tender.

Squeeze the water out of the spinach or chard leaves and put them in the pan. Cook for a few minutes longer until the leaves are soft, folding them in as they become limp. Turn into a serving dish.

Variations: If the broad beans are very young and tender leave them in their pods, top and tail and cut them into 2 or 3 pieces. Or add 500 g (1 lb) jerusalem artichokes or turnips, cut in 2 or 4, at the same time as the broad beans. Or enrich the aromatics with 1 tablespoon of caraway seeds or 1 teaspoon of aniseed and 1 teaspoon of paprika (this will give the dish a North African flavour). Or add a bunch of coriander leaves, chopped coarsely, with the spinach or chard. Or add a pleasant note of colour with a few skinned and chopped tomatoes cooked with the spinach or chard.

TAGINE BETINJAL

Tunisian aubergine tagine   Serves 4

500 g (1 lb) aubergines, diced

1 onion, chopped coarsely

2 tablespoons vegetable oil, plus extra for frying and greasing

2 garlic cloves, crushed

50 g (2 oz) Gruyère or Cheddar cheese, grated

1 hard-boiled egg, chopped

a bunch of fresh parsley, chopped finely

3 eggs, beaten lightly

salt

This egg dish takes its name from the earthenware pot it is cooked in. It is good served hot or cold.

If you have the time, sprinkle the aubergines with salt and leave to drain in a colander for 30 minutes. Rinse and pat dry with kitchen paper.
  Preheat the oven to Gas Mark 8/230°C/ 450°F.
  Fry the onion in the oil until soft. Add more oil and the aubergines and fry, stirring, until soft and lightly coloured. Add a little more oil if necessary and the garlic and fry, stirring, until the aroma rises. Remove the pan from the heat and mix with the rest of the ingredients in a bowl.
  Oil a shallow ovenproof dish and pour in the aubergine mixture. Bake in the oven for 15 minutes or until set.

PUMPKIN WITH RAISINS AND ALMONDS

Serves 6

1.5 kg (3 lb) pumpkin, cubed

2 teaspoons ground cinnamon

1 teaspoon sugar

2 tablespoons raisins or sultanas, soaked in a little water

125 g (4 oz) slivered or flaked almonds, toasted

salt and pepper

This Algerian dish, which sometimes accompanies a simple couscous, is a fine way to use pumpkin.

Cook the pumpkin in a steamer for 15–20 minutes or until tender, or use a pan with a tight-fitting lid and very little water.
  Mash with a fork and season with salt and pepper. Add the cinnamon and sugar and stir in the raisins or sultanas.
  Pour the pumpkin into a flameproof dish and brown lightly under a grill. Sprinkle the almonds over the pumpkin before serving.

FISH

The Mediterranean is not very rich in fish but it offers a great variety. It is all the more curious that not all the countries around the sea make the most of it. I have heard various explanations for this – a chef in Turkey said that in the past people may have thought fish was forbidden by Islam because they did not bleed when they were slit open, and in Morocco I was told that it was because of an ancient fear of the sea and of the things in it.

Turkey and Tunisia have the best fish cookery of the region. Many of the dishes are for any kind of fish – at least that's what they say – which makes it easier to find substitutes for those from the Mediterranean.

L'HOOTZ BCHERMOULA

Fish in Moroccan sauce — Serves 4

750 g (1½ lb) white fish fillets, skinned, e.g. cod, haddock, hake, coley, whiting or monkfish

5 tablespoons olive oil

3 garlic cloves, crushed

1½ teaspoons ground cumin

1 teaspoon paprika

a pinch of chilli powder

a bunch of fresh coriander leaves, chopped finely

salt

juice of 1 lemon, to serve (optional)

Chermoula is the delicious and strongly flavoured sauce – a mixture of herbs and spices with oil – which pervades almost all the fish dishes of Morocco. It varies from town to town and from family to family, but there is always garlic, cumin, paprika, chilli powder and fresh coriander, and often vinegar or lemon. You can use the sauce as a marinade for almost any fish, and cook it in almost any way – by grilling, frying, baking or steaming.

In Morocco a popular way to cook fish is to stew it very slowly on a bed of vegetables (potatoes, turnips, broad beans, peppers or tomatoes). But, by the time the vegetables are done, the fish is generally overcooked. I prefer to cook the fish quickly in the marinade and to stew the vegetables separately.

Cut the chosen fish into 4 cm (1½-inch) cubes. (Monkfish is best cut up when it is cooking and begins to soften.)

Mix together the oil, garlic, cumin, paprika, chilli powder and coriander and salt to taste in a bowl. Add 3 tablespoons of water, and turn the fish in this marinade. Leave for about 1 hour, covered, in a cool place.

Cook the fish for 2–5 minutes (longer for monkfish) in the marinade, turning the pieces over once, until the flesh whitens.

Serve hot or cold, with the lemon juice if you like.

HOUT MIHSHI

Fish stuffed with nuts   Serves 4–6

1 whole fish weighing 1.5 kg (3 lb)

3 tablespoons olive oil, plus extra for greasing

juice of ½ lemon

salt and pepper

For the filling:

2 tablespoons vegetable oil

2 garlic cloves, crushed

2 eggs

1 tablespoon lemon juice

175 g (6 oz) mixed chopped hazelnuts and walnuts

½–1 fresh chilli, chopped finely

a bunch of fresh parsley, chopped finely

salt and pepper

The usual fish for this Tunisian recipe is mullet, but I use salmon trout or bass because I like to bone it. Mullet is too difficult to bone.

Clean the fish but leave the head on. Cut open the belly and release the spine and bones from the flesh with your fingers and a sharp-pointed knife. Break the spine near the head and tail and pull it out.

Preheat the oven to Gas Mark 6/200°C/ 400°F.

To make the filling, heat the oil in a pan and fry the garlic till the aroma rises. Remove the pan from the heat and add the eggs and lemon juice. Stir the mixture over a very low heat until the eggs set in a light cream. Add the nuts, chilli and parsley and salt and pepper to taste.

Pack the fish with this mixture and secure the opening with cocktail sticks. Lightly oil an ovenproof dish, place the fish in it and sprinkle with salt and pepper and the oil and lemon juice. Cover with foil and bake for 30 minutes or until the flesh begins to flake, basting with the juices at least once.

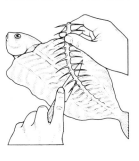

SULTAN IBRAHIM

Red mullet grilled in vine leaves   Serves 6

6 small red mullet

125 ml (4 fl oz) olive oil

4 garlic cloves, crushed

a bunch of fresh parsley,
chopped finely

12 large fresh or preserved
vine leaves

salt and pepper

1½ lemons, cut in wedges,
to garnish

The mullet are impregnated with the flavours of olive oil and garlic, and of the lemony leaves burning over red coals.

Clean and scale the fish, but leave the liver inside – it is a delicacy. Prick each one with a needle in a few places.

Beat the olive oil with the garlic, parsley and salt and pepper and marinate the fish for 1 hour or longer. If using vine leaves preserved in brine, soak them in a few changes of water for 1 hour. Fresh leaves can be used as they are.

Wrap each fish in 2 vine leaves. Grill the fish over a hot charcoal fire, or put the parcels under a hot grill for 5–10 minutes, turning them once. Open a parcel and check that the fish is cooked: the flesh should be opaque and almost flaky.

Place the fish on individual plates and open out the charred leaves. Garnish with lemon wedges and hand round what is left of the marinade.

Sultan Ibrahim (Red mullet grilled in vine leaves)

Mantiq Tmatim (Squid in tomato sauce)

BALIK PILAKISI

Fish plaki

Serves 4–6

5 tablespoons olive oil

1 large spanish onion, chopped

2 garlic cloves, crushed

3 medium-size carrots, diced

½ celeriac weighing about 250 g (8 oz), diced

150 ml (¼ pint) water

1 lemon, cut in slices

1 teaspoon dried thyme

250 g (8 oz) tomatoes, skinned and chopped

1 kg (2 lb) fish steaks, cut into 2 cm (¾-inch) slices

a bunch of fresh parsley, chopped

salt and pepper

Turkish fish plaki is slices of fish cooked with vegetables in a pan and served cold. (The Greek version is a whole fish baked in the oven with fried onions, garlic and tomatoes.) It makes a fresh summer meal and a good buffet dish. Fish such as bass, tuna, grey mullet and swordfish are used in Turkey but any kind of white fish – cod, haddock and halibut – will do.

Heat the oil in a large pan and fry the onion till soft. Add the garlic, carrots and celeriac and stir for about 5 minutes. Pour in the water, lemon slices and thyme and season with salt and pepper. Simmer for 15 minutes or until the vegetables are soft.

Add the tomatoes and put in the fish. Sprinkle over the parsley and simmer gently until the fish is cooked, making sure that it is bathed in the sauce. In Turkey they cook the fish for 25 minutes, but in my view it is better when it just turns white and begins to flake when you prick it with a knife. This can take as little as 5 minutes. Let it cool before serving.

Balik Pilakisi
(Fish plaki)

MANTIQ TMATIM

Squid in tomato sauce   Serves 4

1 kg (2 lb) squid
3 tablespoons olive oil
1 spanish onion, chopped
3 garlic cloves, chopped
500 g (1 lb) tomatoes, skinned and diced
1½ tablespoons wine vinegar
½ teaspoon saffron strands, crushed in a little water (optional)
a bunch of fresh parsley, chopped finely
a bunch of fresh coriander, chopped finely
salt and pepper

Vinegar and saffron make this dish very special.

Clean the squid by pulling the head out of the pouch and with it the soft innards and transparent spine (1). Peel off the reddish membrane from the body and rinse out the mucous membrane from inside. Sever the eyes from the rest of the head (2). Cut the body into rings 1 cm (½ inch) thick and the tentacles into small pieces (3).

Heat the oil in a pan and fry the onion until soft and golden. Add the garlic and fry until it begins to colour, then add the tomatoes, vinegar and saffron, if used. Season with salt and pepper.

Put the squid in the sauce, adding just enough water to cover. Simmer for 4–5 minutes for baby squid or until the squid is tender and opaque – this can take as long as 45 minutes for large squid. You must watch the squid constantly, as the flesh hardens quickly if overcooked.

Add the herbs and serve with bread or on a bed of rice.

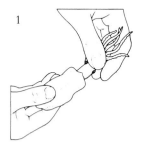

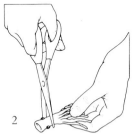

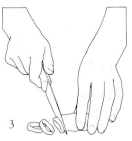

COUIRAT EL HOUT

Fish balls

2 slices of white bread, crusts removed

750 g (1½ lb) cod, haddock, whiting or hake fillets, skinned and chopped or minced

1 large egg (size 1–2)

a bunch of fresh parsley, chopped finely

For the sauce:

3 tablespoons vegetable oil

1 large onion, chopped finely

2 garlic cloves, crushed

397 g (14 oz) can of tomatoes

1 teaspoon paprika

1 teaspoon ground cumin

¼ teaspoon turmeric

a good pinch of chilli powder (optional)

juice of ½ lemon, or more

300 ml (½ pint) water

salt and pepper

All Middle Eastern countries make some kind of fish balls or fingers which are deep-fried or cooked in a sauce. These are Algerian-style and can be served with couscous.

Soak the bread in some water and squeeze dry.

Mix the fish with the egg and parsley. (A food processor will blend the mixture to a paste very quickly but may make it too soft to handle.) Wet your hands and form the fish mixture into little balls the size of a large walnut.

To make the sauce, heat the oil in a large pan and fry the onion until golden. Add the garlic and, when it begins to colour, add the tomatoes, paprika, cumin, turmeric, chilli powder, if using, and lemon juice and salt and pepper to taste. Pour in the water and bring to the boil.

Drop the fish balls into the sauce and simmer for about 8 minutes, turning once.

Serve the fish balls hot or cold, in their sauce.

GAMBARI ALA SHISH

Barbecued prawns   Serves 6

1 kg (2 lb) prawns in their
shells

6 tablespoons olive oil

3 garlic cloves, crushed

1½ teaspoons ground cumin

1½ teaspoons paprika

a good pinch of chilli
powder

juice of 1 lemon

salt

*Only large fleshy prawns – jumbo or king size – are
worth putting on the grill.*

Thread the prawns in their shells onto skewers
and put them over a charcoal fire or under a
hot grill for about 8 minutes, turning once.

Beat together the oil, garlic, cumin, paprika,
chilli powder and lemon juice in a bowl.
Season with salt. Serve the sauce with the
prawns for everyone to dip in.

*Couirat El Hout
(Fish balls)
Gambari Ala Shish
(Barbecued prawns)*

MEAT AND POULTRY

Meat and poultry are interchangeable in many dishes, notably stews which are the mainstay of Middle Eastern cooking. Lamb is preferred, but veal and beef are also used. They are cooked long and slowly to melting tenderness with all kinds of pulses, vegetables and fruit. The art lies in marrying the ingredients happily and in flavouring them with delicacy. They are served with rice, couscous or bulgar wheat, or with bread.

Meatballs, like stews, belong to home cooking, while meats grilled on charcoal are part of the restaurant and street vendors' trade. But it is easy to cook kebabs under the grill or on the barbecue. They are fun to make and to eat, and they make an attractive meal accompanied by salads.

LAHMA BI FOUL AHDAR WA SABANEKH

Beef with broad beans and spinach   Serves 4–6

3 tablespoons olive oil
1 onion, chopped
2 garlic cloves, crushed
500 g (1 lb) beef, cubed
2 dried limes (page 10) or 1 lime
1 kg (2 lb) broad beans, shelled
500 g (1 lb) spinach, rinsed well
salt and pepper

This Egyptian stew can be served with rice or bulgar wheat. The dried limes introduce an Iraqi flavour.

Heat the oil in a pan and fry the onion until golden. Add the garlic and meat and turn to brown it all over. Sprinkle with a little salt and pepper, add the lime(s) and pour in enough water to cover. Simmer, covered, for 45 minutes–1 hour or until tender. Add more water if necessary. Cut the lime(s) open when soft.

Drop the broad beans into the stew and cook for 10 minutes longer. Stir in the spinach and cook for a few minutes more. Serve at once.

DJEJ MIHSHI BIL SEKSU

Chicken with couscous stuffing   Serves 4

3 tablespoons olive oil

1 onion, grated or chopped finely

1 teaspoon ground cinnamon

¼ teaspoon ground ginger

¼ teaspoon saffron strands, crushed in a little water

2 garlic cloves, crushed

1 chicken, weighing about 1.25 kg (3 lb)

300 ml (½ pint) water

2 tablespoons icing sugar (optional)

2 tablespoons clear honey

salt and pepper

For the stuffing:

500 g (1 lb) couscous

450 ml (¾ pint) water

1–2 tablespoons caster sugar (optional)

4 tablespoons vegetable or olive oil

75 g (3 oz) raisins, soaked in water for a few minutes

2 tablespoons orange-flower water (optional)

250 g (8 oz) blanched almonds

50 g (2 oz) shelled pistachios

salt

Traditional recipes say the chicken should be stuffed with steamed couscous and cooked in a spicy sauce, but it is easier, and just as good, to cook and serve the stuffing separately. It is a sweet dish with a fair amount of sugar, which you may prefer to reduce, or omit altogether, but keep the honey in the sauce.

Heat the oil in a large pan and cook the onion until soft. Add the spices and garlic, salt and pepper to taste, and the chicken. Add the water and simmer, covered, for 1 hour or until the chicken is tender, turning it occasionally so it is well impregnated with the sauce.

Preheat the oven to Gas Mark 9/240°C/ 475°F if using it.

Meanwhile, make the stuffing. Put the couscous in a bowl with the water and a little salt. Stir well and let it absorb the water for 10–15 minutes, and then rub with your hands to break up any soggy lumps. Add the sugar, if using, 3 tablespoons of the oil, the raisins and orange-flower water, if using, and stir in with your hands.

Heat the remaining oil and fry the almonds and pistachios until golden. Coarsely chop them and stir into the couscous. Heat the mixture in a pan, adding a little water if not quite tender, and put the lid on.

Take the chicken out of the sauce, sift the icing sugar (if using) over the surface and put it in the oven to caramelise for 15–20 minutes. If you omit this step you may need to cook the chicken longer in the pan.

Boil the sauce to reduce it and stir in the honey.

To serve, put the chicken in the middle of a large round dish. Put a ring of hot stuffing around it and pour the sauce on top.

SOUMANAT BIL EINAB

Quails with grapes

Serves 4

4 quails
3 cm (1½-inch) piece of fresh root ginger
40–50 g (1½–2 oz) butter
1 tablespoon olive oil
1 teaspoon ground cinnamon
250 g (8 oz) white grapes, de-seeded
salt and pepper

This is a Moroccan dish.

Clean the quails. Extract the juice from the ginger by cutting it into pieces and then squeezing the pieces in a garlic press.

Heat the butter and oil in a large pan and sauté the quails very quickly, adding salt and pepper to taste, the cinnamon and the ginger

Djej Mquali (Chicken with lemon and olives)

Djej Mihshi Bil Seksu (Chicken with couscous stuffing)

juice. (In Morocco dried ginger powder is used, but the juice gives a fresher taste.) Turn the quails to brown them all over.

Add the grapes and cook, covered, for 10 minutes, turning the quails once more. Serve hot.

Soumanat Bil Einab
(Quails with grapes)

DJEJ MQUALI

Chicken with lemon and olives   Serves 4

2 tablespoons olive or
vegetable oil

1 large onion, chopped
coarsely

1 garlic clove, crushed

¼ teaspoon ground ginger

¼ teaspoon saffron strands,
crushed in a little water

150 ml (¼ pint) water

1 chicken, with giblets
(optional), jointed

50–75 g (2–3 oz) Greek
calamata olives

1–2 preserved lemons (page
11), pulp removed, chopped

salt

*The flavour of lemons which have lost their sharpness
through preservation in salt belongs to Morocco where
it pervades many cooked dishes and salads. At every
vegetable market you can see stalls laden with huge
piles of soft lemons oozing with juice beside several
varieties of olives. The two are often used together, as
they are in this dish. Making your own preserved
lemons is very easy.*

*In Morocco a chicken dish is more highly esteemed
if the bird comes to the table whole, but when its
excellence depends on long slow cooking in
flavoursome juices it makes more sense to cut it up
into pieces and to have them soaking in the sauce.*

Heat the oil in a large heavy-based saucepan
and fry the onion until soft. Add the garlic,
ginger, and saffron and pour in the water. Put
in the chicken pieces and the chicken liver, if
using, and cook very gently, covered, until the
chicken is so tender that the flesh comes off the
bone when you pull it. Turn the chicken
frequently and add more water if necessary.

Soak the olives in water for 15 minutes and
then boil in fresh water for another 2 minutes.

Lift out the chicken pieces and reserve.
Mash the liver, if using, or put it through a
blender with some of the onions and then
return it to the pan (it is meant to enrich the
sauce). Add a little salt. Reduce the sauce
further if necessary until it has a rich thick
consistency.

Add the preserved lemon peel to the sauce.
Put the chicken back into the saucepan to heat
it through.

Serve the chicken with the sauce, with the
olives poured over the top.

Variation: An Algerian version which you
might like to try has 2 or 3 tomatoes, skinned
and chopped, put in at the start, and a bunch of
fresh coriander, chopped coarsely, added
towards the end.

DJEJ MATISHA MESLA

Chicken tagine with onions and tomatoes   Serves 4

3 tablespoons vegetable oil

3 onions, grated

4 chicken quarters

1 kg (2 lb) tomatoes, skinned and chopped

¼ teaspoon ground ginger

2 teaspoons ground cinnamon

½ teaspoon saffron strands, crushed in a little water (optional)

2 tablespoons clear honey

2 tablespoons sesame seeds, toasted (optional)

salt and pepper

In this Moroccan dish, the chicken cooks in the juice of fresh tomatoes and onions and is sweetened at the end with honey.

Heat the oil in a large pan and fry the onions and chicken until lightly browned. Add the tomatoes, spices, saffron, if using, and salt and pepper to taste. Cook gently, covered, turning the chicken pieces over occasionally, until the flesh is so tender it can be pulled off the bone easily.

Remove the chicken, and reduce the sauce to a thick sizzling cream. Stir as it begins to caramelise and be careful that it does not stick or burn. Stir in the honey, return the chicken pieces to the sauce and heat through.

Serve the chicken covered with the sauce and, if you like, sprinkled with the sesame seeds.

SHISH TAOUK

Skewered chicken pieces   Serves 4

4 tablespoons olive oil

2–4 garlic cloves, crushed

juice of ½ lemon

4 boneless chicken breasts,
cut into 2 cm (¾-inch)
pieces

melted butter for basting
(optional)

salt and pepper

To garnish:

a bunch of fresh parsley,
chopped coarsely

1 lemon, cut into wedges

*A lovely dish; the main thing is not to overcook the
chicken but to keep it moist because it can so easily
dry out. The breast is the traditional cut, but meat
from the leg is juicier; you may prefer it.*

Mix the oil, garlic, lemon juice and a little
pepper in a bowl, and place the chicken pieces
in this marinade for 1 hour or longer.

Lift out the meat and sprinkle a little salt
over it before threading onto skewers
(preferably wide, flat-bladed ones to prevent
the chicken from sliding). Turn over a
medium-hot fire or under a medium-hot grill
for 6–10 minutes, brushing frequently with the
marinade or with melted butter, if preferred.

Serve at once, straight onto plates or on a
serving dish, on a bed of parsley garnished with
lemon wedges.

Variations: Instead of garlic use an onion,
minced in a blender, and 1 teaspoon of ground
cinnamon. This idea comes from Turkey. Or
try *Joujeh* kebab – an Iranian version – add a
good pinch of saffron, crushed and mixed with
the juice of ½ lemon, salt and pepper and 3
tablespoons of melted butter. Or mix 1
teaspoon of paprika and a pinch of chilli
powder with salt and pepper in 4 tablespoons
of olive oil. Serve sprinkled with chopped fresh
coriander. I found this recipe in Morocco.

KOFTA KEBAB

Minced meat on skewers (Pictured on front cover)   Serves 6

1 kg (2 lb) boneless lamb,
preferably from the shoulder

2 onions, grated

1 teaspoon ground
cinnamon

½ teaspoon ground allspice

*This dish is exquisitely aromatic and deliciously soft,
but you must be very careful not to dry it out in
cooking.*

*If you do not have skewers, shape the meat into
burgers.*

a pinch of chilli powder (optional)

a large bunch of fresh parsley, chopped finely

a few sprigs of fresh mint, chopped finely

oil for brushing

salt and pepper

To garnish:

fresh parsley

1 lemon, cut into wedges

If the meat is lean, add quite a bit of fat to keep it moist and juicy (most of it will melt away). Cut the meat and fat into small pieces. Place them in a food processor with the onions, spices, chilli powder, if using, herbs and salt and pepper and blend well. If you do not have a food processor use minced lamb and work it and the seasonings to a soft consistency with your hands.

Divide the meat into 6 portions. Wet your hands, take each portion and wrap it around a skewer with a wide flat blade. Shape into a sausage about 12 cm (5 inches) long and press firmly so that it holds together without sliding on the skewer. Oil the grill. Place the skewers on the grill and turn over hot embers for 5–8 minutes. Alternatively, cook the kebabs on a tray under a hot grill.

Serve at once, on a bed of parsley on individual plates or on a serving dish. Garnish with the lemon wedges and serve with warm pitta bread and salads.

Variation: A good way of serving this kebab is on a bed of strained sheep's milk yogurt or greek yogurt. Warm up, but do not boil, 1.5 litres (3 pints) of yogurt. Pour onto the serving plate or onto each individual plate, and place the meat on top. Mix 1 tablespoon of paprika with 2 tablespoons of olive oil and dribble over the dish. Toast or fry 2 tablespoons of pine kernels and sprinkle over the top. Garnish with chopped fresh parsley.

KEFTA TAGINE

Meatballs in tomato sauce with eggs   Serves 6

For the sauce:

3 tablespoons vegetable oil

1½ large onions, chopped

2 garlic cloves, crushed

750 g (1½ lb) tomatoes, skinned and chopped

These hot spicy meatballs in tomato sauce, topped with eggs, are Moroccan. Serve them as a delicious starter or as a main course.

To prepare the sauce, heat the oil in a wide, flameproof casserole and fry the onions until golden. Add the garlic and, when the aroma rises, add the tomatoes, spices and parsley and

1 teaspoon ground paprika

½ teaspoon ground cumin

½ teaspoon ground cinnamon

a bunch of fresh parsley, chopped finely

300 ml (½ pint) water

salt

For the meatballs:

750 g (1½ lb) minced lamb or veal

a small bunch of fresh parsley, chopped finely

a small bunch of fresh coriander, chopped finely

a few fresh mint leaves or 2 teaspoons dried mint

1 teaspoon ground paprika

1 teaspoon ground cumin

1 teaspoon ground cinnamon

¼ teaspoon ground ginger

salt

To finish:

6 eggs

salt to taste. Stir in the water and simmer for 15 minutes.

Meanwhile, mix together the meat, herbs, spices and salt to taste and work them to a paste with your hands. Wet your hands and roll the mixture into marble-sized balls.

Drop the meatballs into the sauce and simmer for 15 minutes. Not long before you are ready to serve, break the eggs onto the simmering stew and cook for 10 minutes. They will stay on the surface and the dish will be ready when they are set. Do not let them become too firm.

ARNAB MUKHALAL

Rabbit with vinegar   Serves 4

3–4 tablespoons olive oil

about 500 g (1 lb) rabbit portions, cut into pieces

500 g (1 lb) small whole onions, or 2 large onions, chopped coarsely

1 garlic clove, crushed

500 g (1 lb) tomatoes, skinned and chopped

In the Muslim world where alcohol is forbidden, vinegar is used in cooking where wine would be used in other countries. It gives this dish a rich, strong flavour. But start with the smaller quantity and add more later to taste.

Heat the oil in a large casserole and brown the rabbit pieces. Take them out and fry the onions in the same oil until golden, then add the garlic.

75–150 ml (3–5 fl oz) red wine vinegar

½ teaspoon ground allspice

1 teaspoon ground cinnamon

1 cardamom pod, cracked

1 tablespoon sugar

2–3 tablespoons currants

a small bunch of fresh parsley, chopped finely

salt and pepper

Return the rabbit pieces to the casserole and add the tomatoes. Pour in the vinegar and add salt and pepper to taste, and the allspice, cinnamon, cardamom and sugar. Add enough water to cover the rabbit. Cover and simmer for 1½ hours or until the rabbit is very tender.

Add the currants and parsley towards the end of cooking. Stir well. Remove the lid and continue cooking to reduce the sauce until it is thick and creamy.

Serve with plain rice or bulgar wheat.

Note: You may also cook the rabbit in an oven preheated to Gas Mark 4/180°C/350°F for about 2 hours.

COUSCOUS

Serves 10–12

For the stew:

1 kg (2 lb) leg, shoulder or fillet of lamb, cut into pieces and trimmed of excess fat

50 g (2 oz) butter or 3 tablespoons sunflower oil

½ teaspoon ground ginger

2 teaspoons ground cinnamon

500 g (1 lb) stoned prunes

2–3 tablespoons clear honey (optional)

salt and pepper

For the chick-peas:

250 g (8 oz) chick-peas, soaked for 2 hours and drained

500 g (1 lb) seedless raisins

salt

For the soup and sauce:

500 g (1 lb) small onions

In restaurants a couscous meal is presented in many parts all in different serving bowls. There is a large bowl of the grain, a kind of semolina called couscous, one of chick-peas and raisins, a third with a rich vegetable soup, a fourth with stewed meat or chicken, and a small bowl of hot peppery sauce. Brochettes (kebabs) and kefta (meatballs) are sometimes provided as an alternative to the meat stew. It all sounds very elaborate and of course there are many ingredients, but it does constitute an entire meal for a lot of people and is really very easy to make. Everything can be done in advance except for the grain, which should be started about half an hour before serving.

To make the stew, brown the meat in the butter or oil. Add the spices and water to cover and season with salt and pepper. Simmer, covered, for 2–3 hours or until the meat is so tender you can pull it apart. Add more water if necessary. Add the prunes and honey, if using, stir well and cook a few minutes longer.

For the chick-peas and raisins, put the chick-peas in a pan, cover with water and simmer for about 1½ hours, adding water to keep them covered and salt when they are tender. Add the raisins about 15 minutes before the end.

500 g (1 lb) carrots, cut in ½ lengthways
500 g (1 lb) aubergines, cut into large pieces
about 2.75 litres (5 pints) water
½ teaspoon ground ginger
2 teaspoons ground cinnamon
½ teaspoon saffron strands, crushed in a little water (optional)
250 g (8 oz) potatoes, quartered
500 g (1 lb) turnips, halved or quartered
500 g (1 lb) shelled broad beans
250 g (8 oz) tomatoes, skinned
500 g (1 lb) white cabbage, cut into slices
500 g (1 lb) pumpkin, cubed, or courgettes, sliced into 4
a large bunch of fresh coriander, chopped coarsely
2 teaspoons paprika
½ teaspoon chilli powder, or more
salt and pepper
For the grain:
1 kg (2 lb) packet of couscous
about 1.2 litres (2 pints) lightly salted water
4 tablespoons sunflower oil
65–75 g (2½–3 oz) butter or 4 tablespoons oil

For the vegetable soup, put the onions, carrots and aubergines in a large pan with the water. Add the spices and saffron, if using, and salt and pepper and simmer for 1 hour. Add the potatoes, turnips, broad beans and tomatoes and simmer for 20 minutes longer. Add the cabbage and pumpkin or courgettes and simmer for a further 20 minutes or until the vegetables are tender. Finally, add the coriander and cook a moment more.

For the peppery sauce, take a few ladlefuls of the stock from the vegetable soup and stir in the paprika and chilli powder to taste.

For the grain, put the couscous in a large bowl. Pour in about half the quantity of water and stir well until evenly absorbed. Leave for 10 minutes. Add the rest of the water and the sunflower oil and rub the couscous between your palms to make sure that it does not stick together in lumps. Leave for about 10 minutes until it is swollen and tender but with the grains still separate. Steam the couscous, uncovered, to heat through, or heat it up in a saucepan or, covered, in the oven. Transfer to a serving dish, break up any lumps with a fork and stir in the butter or oil.

To serve, pass around the bowls of couscous, chick-peas, soup, stew and sauce for everyone to help themselves.

Couscous

MISHMISHEYA

Lamb stew with apricots (Pictured on page 4)   Serves 8

3 tablespoons olive oil

2 onions, cut in half and sliced

1 kg (2 lb) lamb (shoulder or fillet), trimmed of fat and cubed

250 g (8 oz) chick-peas, soaked for 1 hour and drained

3 teaspoons ground cinnamon

750 g (1½ lb) fresh apricots, halved and stones removed

salt and pepper

Sugar is usually added as well as a handful of raisins to this delicate cinnamon-flavoured Tunisian dish, but I have left them out as the apricots are sweet enough.

It is easy to make in large quantities for a party and you can make it in advance and reheat it gently.

Heat the oil in a pan and fry the onions until golden. Add the meat and turn to brown it all over. Add the chick-peas, pour in enough water to cover and bring to the boil. Remove any scum, add a little pepper and the cinnamon and simmer for an hour or until the meat and chick-peas are very tender. Do not add salt until the chick-peas have begun to soften.

Add the apricots and cook for a further 20 minutes; they should be really soft. Serve the stew with plain rice or couscous.

KHORESH ALOU

Meat and prune stew   Serves 6

3 tablespoons sunflower oil

2 onions, chopped

750 g (1½ lb) stewing lamb or beef, cubed

2 dried limes (page 10) or 1 lime

250 g (8 oz) stoned prunes

500 g (1 lb) spinach, rinsed well and shredded

1 bunch of spring onions, chopped finely

salt and pepper

This fruity Iranian stew has the special mellow flavour of dried limes. Serve it hot with plain rice.

Heat the oil in a pan and fry the onions until golden. Add the meat and brown it all over. Season with salt and pepper, add the lime(s), pour in enough water to cover and simmer very gently for 1½ hours or until the meat is tender, adding more water as necessary. As soon as the lime(s) are soft enough, pierce with the point of a knife to release their flavour.

Add the prunes, spinach and spring onions and cook for 30 minutes longer. Serve at once.

SHISH KEBAB

Skewered meats   Serves 6

*150 ml (¼ pint) olive oil,
plus extra for greasing*

2 onions, grated

4 bay leaves, crushed

*2 tablespoons dried mint or
marjoram*

*1 kg (2 lb) leg of lamb, or
beef (sirloin, fillet or rump
steak), cut into 2 cm (¾-
inch) cubes*

salt and pepper

To garnish:

2 lemons, cut in wedges

*a bunch of fresh parsley or
mint*

*Lamb is the usual meat for kebabs, but beef is also
used. Although presentation is more attractive with
tomatoes, onions and peppers interspersed with bay
leaves between the cubes of meat, the cooking is more
successful if there is only meat on the skewers.*

Mix the oil, onions, herbs and a little pepper in
a bowl and soak the meat in this marinade for
at least 1 hour or overnight, turning the pieces
over once.

Lift out the meat, sprinkle with a little salt
and thread on long, flat-bladed skewers.

Oil a grill, add the meat and place it about
7 cm (3 inches) from the embers of a wood or
charcoal fire. Cook quickly – lamb for 7–10
minutes, less for beef (it is best rare) – turning
over once, so that the outside is well browned
while the inside is pink and juicy. Alternatively,
cook on a tray under a medium-hot grill.

Serve garnished with lemon wedges and
sprigs of parsley or mint. Accompany by Salata
Baladi (Mixed Salad Arab-style, page 27) and
warm pitta bread.

TERBIYELI KEREVIZ

Lamb and celeriac stew   Serves 4

3 tablespoons olive oil

2 onions, cut in half and sliced thinly

500 g (1 lb) lean fillet or leg of lamb, cut in pieces

2 celeriac, weighing about 1.25 kg (2½ lb), cut into quarters

2 egg yolks

juice of ½ lemon

salt and pepper

Kofta Bi Bamia (Meatballs with okra)

Shish Kebab (Skewered meats)

A delicate Turkish stew with an egg and lemon sauce.

Heat the oil in a pan and fry the onions until soft. Add the meat and stir to brown all over.

Add the celeriac, season with salt and pepper, and pour in enough water to cover. Simmer, covered, for about 1 hour or until the meat is very tender. As soon as the celeriac is tender, lift it out and cut it into sticks. When the meat is done, put the celeriac back into the pan for a few minutes until it is soft.

Just before you are ready to serve, beat the egg yolks with the lemon juice and a few tablespoons of the cooking liquid. Pour this sauce into the pan and stir for a minute or so until the sauce thickens, but do not let it boil. Serve hot.

Terbiyeli Kereviz (Lamb and celeriac stew)

KOFTA BI BAMIA

Meatballs with okra   Serves 4

500 g (1 lb) okra
500 g (1 lb) minced lamb
1 teaspoon ground cinnamon
¼ teaspoon ground allspice
2 tablespoons chopped fresh parsley
3 tablespoons oil
1 large onion, sliced thinly
1 garlic clove, sliced
3 large tomatoes, skinned and chopped
juice of ½ lemon (optional)
salt and pepper

Wash the okra and trim the stems but do not cut through the pod or the gelatinous juice will come out in cooking.

Mix together the meat, cinnamon, allspice, parsley and salt and pepper to taste and work well with your hands into a soft paste. Roll into small balls the size of a large hazelnut.

Heat the oil in a large pan and fry the onion until soft. Add the garlic and the meatballs and fry, shaking and turning the meatballs so they colour all over.

Add the okra and tomatoes, a little salt and pepper and enough water just to cover. Simmer, with the lid on, for about 25 minutes or until the okra are tender.

Stir in the lemon juice, if using. Serve hot, with rice or bulgar wheat.

KIBBEH BIL SANNIEH

Kibbeh in a tray   Serves 12

For the crust:

500 g (1 lb) bulgar wheat
1 onion
1 kg (2 lb) lean tender lamb, preferably from the leg, or minced lamb
1 teaspoon ground cinnamon
1 teaspoon ground allspice
a good pinch of chilli powder
5 tablespoons olive oil, plus extra for greasing
salt and pepper

This kind of meat pie – with a bulgar wheat and meat paste (called kibbeh*) for a crust – is a well-known Lebanese and Syrian dish. It is easy to prepare in large quantities.*

To make the crust, put the bulgar wheat in a bowl and cover with cold water for 20 minutes. (It will have absorbed some water but will still be hard.) Rinse in a sieve.

Put the onion through a food processor, then add the meat and spices and salt and pepper to taste and chop to a paste. Now blend the bulgar wheat with the lamb mixture. To achieve a very soft homogeneous paste, you will have to do it in batches and you may need to add cold water a tablespoonful at a time.

If you do not have a food processor, grate the onion and pound with the minced lamb, spices and bulgar wheat, or work it vigorously

For the filling:

2 tablespoons vegetable or olive oil

1 large onion, chopped finely

3 tablespoons pine kernels

500 g (1 lb) minced beef

1 teaspoon ground cinnamon

½ teaspoon ground allspice

2 tablespoons currants

salt and pepper

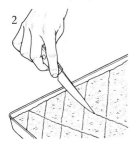

with your hands.

Preheat the oven to Gas Mark 6/200°C/400°F.

To prepare the filling, heat the oil in a pan and fry the onion until soft. Add the pine kernels and fry until golden. Add the meat, seasonings and currants and cook, stirring, for about 10 minutes.

Now assemble the pie. Oil a large shallow baking sheet about 35 × 40 cm (14 × 16 inches). Wet your hands and spread half the kibbeh mixture on the bottom. Spread the filling evenly over it, then cover with the remaining kibbeh mixture, pressing it down (1).

With a sharp knife, cut deep (but not right through to the bottom), parallel lines 1–2 cm (½–¾ inch) apart, then cross them with diagonal lines to make diamond shapes (2). Sprinkle with the oil and bake for 45–50 minutes or until brown.

Serve hot or cold (hot is best), accompanied by yogurt and a salad.

SIKBAJ

Lamb with aubergines and dates   Serves 6–8

750 g (1½ lb) aubergines,
cubed

3 tablespoons olive oil

2 large onions, cut in half
and sliced

750 g (1½ lb) lean lamb,
cubed

1 teaspoon ground
cinnamon

½ teaspoon ground allspice

¼ teaspoon ground ginger

175 g (6 oz) dried dates,
stones removed

4–5 tablespoons wine
vinegar

2 tablespoons rose-water

salt and pepper

125 g (4 oz) blanched
almonds, toasted, to garnish

*A mixture of puréed dates and vinegar (a combination
that has come down from ancient Persia to the
countries of North Africa) gives a wonderful sweet
and sour flavour to this aromatic stew. It is very easy
to make in large quantities.*

Place the aubergines in a colander, sprinkle
with salt and leave for 30 minutes. Rinse the
salt off and drain.

Heat the oil in a large pan and fry the onions
until golden. Add the meat and turn to brown
it all over. Add the cinnamon, allspice, ginger
and a little pepper and cover with water. Bring
to the boil, remove any scum and then simmer
for 1 hour or until the meat is tender. Add the
aubergines and cook for 30 minutes longer.

Put the dates with the vinegar and a little
water in a blender. Purée to make a thick
'cream' consistency, adding more water if
necessary. Pour this sauce over the stew.
Sprinkle with the rose-water and cook for a
few minutes longer.

Serve hot, garnished with the almonds.

LABAN IMMO

Lamb in yogurt sauce   Serves 6

750 g (1½ lb) lean tender
lamb, cut from the leg or
fillet, cubed

250 g (8 oz) small onions

1 cinnamon stick

900 ml (1½ pints) sheep's
milk yogurt or strained
yogurt

2 tablespoons cornflour

1 tablespoon dried mint

2 garlic cloves, crushed
(optional)

salt and pepper

This is an Arab dish. The name literally means 'his mother's milk', the image being that of a young lamb cooked in yogurt made from sheep's milk. Serve with rice or bulgar wheat.

Put the meat in a pan with just enough water to cover. Bring to the boil and remove the scum. Add the onions, cinnamon stick and salt and pepper, and simmer for about 45 minutes until the meat is tender, adding more water if necessary.

Heat the yogurt in another pan. Before it gets too hot, mix the cornflour with a few tablespoons of water in a cup and stir it into the yogurt to stabilise and prevent it from curdling; it also thickens the sauce. Stir constantly as the yogurt comes to the boil and begins to thicken.

Add the mint and garlic, if using, stir well, and pour over the meat. Cook gently for about 10 minutes longer.

Variation: Fresh broad beans can be thrown in 15 minutes before adding the yogurt.

GRAINS, PASTA AND PULSES

Apart from North Africa where couscous (a kind of semolina of Berber origin) is the staple food, a bowl of rice comes with the main meal in most Middle Eastern cities. In the countryside, wheat, either bulgar or whole, pasta or beans (brown in Egypt, white in Turkey) takes its place.

All of these are embellished with herbs and spices, with garnishes and by mixing with all kinds of other ingredients.

ROZ

Plain rice   Serves 4–6

500 g (1 lb) long-grain rice

3 tablespoons vegetable oil

750 ml (1¼ pints) water

salt

There are different kinds of rice in the Middle East ranging from long-grain and round (which is used for fillings and for puddings) to the very thin grain of Iran and Iraq. Each country has its own special way of cooking it and each requires a different quantity of water. This is one of the simplest ways.

Soak the rice in salted water for at least an hour. This gets rid of the fine powder which makes it sticky. Drain well.

Heat the oil in a heavy-based or non-stick saucepan. Throw in the rice and stir until it becomes transparent (this helps to keep it separate). Pour in the water and stir in a little salt. Bring to the boil and then cook, covered, on the lowest possible heat for about 20 minutes. If you use a non-stick pan you can turn it out like a cake.

KETCHRI

Red lentils and rice   Serves 6

500 g (1 lb) basmati rice

250 g (8 oz) red lentils

5 tablespoons olive oil

2 tablespoons tomato purée

1 litre (1¾ pints) water

½ teaspoon turmeric

2 garlic cloves, crushed

3 teaspoons ground cumin

salt and pepper

This spicy Iraqi dish makes a meal with yogurt. It usually oozes with butter which gives a delicious flavour. But on occasions it is made with oil for serving with meat or chicken. I give the lighter method.

Wash the rice and soak it in salted water for at least 1 hour. Pick over and wash the lentils. Drain both.

Heat 2 tablespoons of the oil in a heavy-based or non-stick pan and stir in the tomato purée and water. Add the turmeric and a little salt and pepper to taste and stir well. When it comes to the boil, add the rice and lentils. Cook, covered, on the lowest possible heat for 30 minutes.

Heat the remaining oil and cook the garlic quickly until barely coloured. Stir in the cumin and, when the aroma rises, pour over the rice and lentils and mix in with a fork. Cover the rice and steam for another 10 minutes, adding more water if necessary.

HUMMUS WA SABANEKH

Chick-peas and spinach   Serves 6

175 g (6 oz) chick-peas,
soaked for 1 hour

1 kg (2 lb) fresh spinach,
rinsed well and shredded if
wished

4 tablespoons olive oil

4–5 garlic cloves, crushed

1½ teaspoons ground
coriander

salt and pepper

*This vegetable dish may also be made with meatballs.
Its flavour comes from the fried garlic and coriander.
This particular flavouring is Egyptian.*

Drain the chick-peas. Cook them in enough
water to cover for about an hour or until they
are tender, adding salt when they begin to
soften. Keep them covered with water but let it
reduce a little, or drain most of it off when
they are done.

Add the spinach to the chick-peas and stir
until softened. Add pepper to taste.

Now make this very Egyptian sauce called
taklia. Heat the oil in a pan and fry the garlic
with the coriander until the aroma rises.

Stir the sauce into the chick-pea and spinach
mixture. Heat through and serve.

Variation: Fry a chopped onion in 2
tablespoons of oil, add the spinach and stir
until it crumples into a soft mass. Sprinkle with
salt and pepper and add the boiled and drained
chick-peas and 4 skinned and chopped
tomatoes. Heat through until the tomatoes
soften.

Note: You can use a 432 g (15 oz) can of
chick-peas instead of dried.

*Hummus Wa Sabanekh
(Chick-peas and spinach)
Ketchri (Red lentils
and rice)*

BASMATI STEAMED RICE

500 g (1 lb) basmati rice

3 tablespoons salt

75 g (3 oz) butter

The best quality long-grain rice you can buy here is basmati, which is small and thin and comes from India and Pakistan. It remains firm and separate when cooked and has an enchanting flavour and aroma. My favourite way of cooking it – partially boiled and then left to steam in the saucepan – is inspired by, but less perfectionist than, the Iranian way. It is very easy; once you get used to it you will never fail to make perfect rice.

Wash the rice in a colander (this removes the starchy powder which makes it sticky) and then put it in a bowl of warm, not hot, water with 1 tablespoon of the salt (it does not penetrate the rice but helps to keep it separate). Leave it to soak for 1 hour or longer.

Bring plenty of water to the boil in a saucepan and add the remaining salt (it still does not make the rice salty). Drain the rice, sprinkle it into the water and let it boil vigorously for 4–6 minutes. Take a grain and test it – it must be still a little hard. Drain quickly.

Put half the butter in the bottom of the empty pan, put the rice on top, add the rest of the butter and stir well. Put the pan on the lowest possible heat with the lid on and let it steam for 20–30 minutes. Serve hot.

Note: You can use oil instead of butter.

BURGHUL

Bulgar wheat   Serves 4

500 g (1 lb) bulgar wheat

1.2 litres (2 pints) water

40 g (1½ oz) butter

1 tablespoon vegetable oil

salt

Bulgar wheat is the staple of Turkey and the part of the Arab world which was called the Fertile Crescent. It is nourishing and very easy to prepare. Many recipes for burghul pilaf combine it with meat or chicken and other ingredients. This one is the simplest. Use it to accompany any of the main dishes and as an alternative to rice.

Wash and drain the bulgar wheat. Bring the water to the boil, add a little salt and pour in the grain. Cook, covered, for 10–15 minutes or until it is tender and the water has been absorbed. Add a little more water if necessary.

Stir the butter and oil into the bulgar wheat and let it rest for a few minutes before serving.

Variations: If you have meat or chicken stock use it instead of water. It will make the best possible bulgar wheat. Or add pulses, such as boiled chick-peas and brown lentils, while it is cooking. Or add fried onions and pine kernels: brown the onions in the butter and oil, add the pine kernels and stir, then add the bulgar wheat, water or stock and salt.

MUJADARA BIL BURGHUL

Lentils and bulgar wheat (Pictured on page 5)   Serves 4–6

250 g (8 oz) green or brown lentils

about 750 ml (1¼ pints) water

125 g (4 oz) bulgar wheat

5 tablespoons olive oil or vegetable oil

1 large spanish onion, cut in half and sliced thinly

salt and pepper

This Syrian dish can be eaten hot or cold (use olive oil if you are going to eat it cold), as an accompaniment to meat or chicken, or as a main dish with yogurt, spring onions, radishes and Salata Baladi (Mixed salad Arab-style, page 27).

Wash the lentils. Put them in a pan with the water and simmer for 10–15 minutes.

Add the bulgar wheat and salt and pepper and cook, covered, on a very low heat for a further 15 minutes until the wheat is plump and tender, adding more water if necessary.

Meanwhile, heat 2 tablespoons of the oil and fry the onion, stirring constantly, until it is so brown that it is almost caramelised. Stir half into the lentil and wheat mixture and add the remaining oil.

Serve garnished with the remaining onion.

DJAVAR POLO

Iranian jewel-encrusted rice   Serves 6–8

1 chicken, weighing about
1.5 kg (3½ lb)

3 tablespoons oil

50 g (2 oz) candied orange
peel, or 2 oranges plus 4
tablespoons sugar (optional)

75 g (3 oz) butter

3 large carrots, grated
coarsely

1 teaspoon ground
cinnamon

2 tablespoons raisins

2 tablespoons currants

¼ teaspoon saffron strands,
crushed and mixed with 1
tablespoon water (optional)

4 tablespoons flaked
almonds

4 tablespoons pistachios, cut
in half lengthways

500 g (1 lb) long-grain
rice, soaked in salted water
for at least 1 hour

salt and pepper

*The 'jewels' in this beautiful chicken and rice dish are
a multi-coloured assortment of nuts and bits of carrot.
When candied orange peel is added the dish is called*
shirin *(sweet)* polo. *Make it for special occasions as
it takes some time to prepare.*

Preheat the oven to Gas Mark 4/180°C/350°F.

Lay the chicken on a large sheet of foil,
season with salt and pepper and rub in 2
tablespoons of the oil with your hands. Wrap
the chicken and bake for 1½ hours or until
very tender and the juices which come out of a
thigh when pricked with a fork are no longer
pink.

If you want to make it a sweet (*shirin*) *polo*,
cut the candied orange peel into thin strips and
reserve. To make your own candied peel,
remove only the orange part of the rind from
the oranges and leave the white part which is
bitter. Cut the rind into strips or chop it in a
food processor. Blanch it twice, each time in
clean water, to remove the bitterness. Add the
sugar, cover with water and simmer until the
syrup thickens (be careful that it does not
caramelise and become hard). Reserve.

Melt half the butter and the remaining oil in
a large frying pan, add the carrots with a little
salt and the cinnamon and sauté, stirring often,
for 10 minutes or until soft. Add the orange
peel, if using, raisins, currants and saffron, if
using. Cook for 5 minutes and then add the
almonds and pistachios.

Drain the rice and sprinkle into boiling
salted water. Let it boil vigorously for 4–8
minutes until it is almost tender (bite a grain –
it should still be a little hard). Watch that it
does not become soft (it can do so very
suddenly). Drain quickly and then return the
rice to the pan. Add the remaining butter and
stir in two-thirds of the carrot and nut mixture.
Put the pan on a very low heat with the lid on

*Djavar Polo (Iranian
jewel-encrusted rice)*

and let it steam for 20 minutes or until the rice is tender.

When you are ready to serve, skin and bone the chicken and cut it into pieces. Pour half the rice mixture onto a large, flat serving plate, spread the chicken pieces on top and cover with the rest of the rice. Pour the chicken juices all over and garnish with the remaining carrot and nut mixture. Everything must be very hot.

Variation: This recipe can be made with meatballs instead of chicken. Work 650 g (1¼ lb) of minced lamb with a small grated onion, ½ teaspoon of ground cinnamon and salt and pepper and roll into marble-sized balls. Fry in a little oil for 8–10 minutes, shaking the pan to brown them all over. Arrange them between two layers of the rice.

ROZ BIL SHAGHRIA

Rice with vermicelli   Serves 4

250 g (8 oz) long-grain rice

125 g (4 oz) vermicelli

450 ml (¾ pint) water

40 g (1½ oz) butter

salt

This way of cooking rice is very popular in the Arab world.

Wash and drain the rice. Break the vermicelli into small pieces with your hands, put it in a tray under a grill and let it become brown.

Bring the water to the boil and add a little salt. Throw in the rice and vermicelli, stir well and cook, covered, for 15 minutes or until both are tender and the water has been absorbed. You may need to add a little more water.

Stir in the butter and serve.

DESSERTS AND PASTRIES

Puddings and pastries are not part of a Middle Eastern meal where the dessert is always fruit. They are for entertaining, for serving with tea and coffee and for special occasions. They are made in great quantities during holiday seasons and religious festivals and for weddings, engagements and to celebrate such events as a homecoming, a birth or a first tooth. But there is no reason why you should not serve them as a dessert. I have chosen only a few.

ORANGE SLICES

(Pictured on title page)   Serves 4

6 oranges

2 tablespoons orange-flower water or orange liqueur

3 teaspoons ground cinnamon

This is a Moroccan salad.

Peel the oranges with a sharp knife, remove all the pith and then cut them into thin slices. Arrange on a serving plate. Sprinkle with the orange-flower water or liqueur and dust with the cinnamon.

M'HENCHA

Moroccan almond snake   Serves 15

550 g (1 lb 2 oz) ground almonds

375 g (12 oz) caster sugar

1 tablespoon ground cinnamon

90–125 ml (3–4 fl oz) orange-flower water or rose-water

400 g (13 oz) packet of fillo pastry

75–125 g (3–4 oz) butter, melted

M'hencha *means snake. It looks beautiful and tastes wonderful and you can make it as large as you like. Fillo can be used instead of the Moroccan pancake-like pastry called* ouarka. *The quantities given make one that is big enough for a party.*

Mix together the ground almonds, sugar, cinnamon and orange-flower water or rose-water (just enough for it to be like moist sand) and work into a paste with your hands.

Preheat the oven to Gas Mark 4/180°C/350°F.

Take the sheets of fillo out only when you

2 egg yolks, beaten with
1 tablespoon water

To garnish:

icing sugar for dusting

1 tablespoon ground
cinnamon

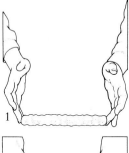

are ready to start, and keep them in a stack while you are working, as they dry out quickly.

Brush the top fillo sheet lightly with butter and flip over to the sheet underneath. Brush again with butter. Take lumps of the almond paste, roll into fingers and place them end to end on the sheet to make a line as thick as a fat thumb about 2.5 cm (1 inch) from the long edge. Roll up the pastry tightly over the almond filling.

Press the ends of the roll towards the centre, like an accordion, so that it becomes crinkled (1) (this ensures that the pastry does not tear when you curve it round). Lift the roll up very carefully and place it on a large sheet of foil (it will make it easier for you to slide it off later) on a large baking sheet. Starting from the centre of the sheet, curve the almond-filled roll into a tight coil (2).

Repeat with the rest of the fillo until all the filling is used up. Place the rolls end to end to make a long curled-up snake (3). Brush the top of the pastry with the egg yolk mixture and bake for about 30 minutes or until crisp and brown.

Dust with icing sugar and sprinkle lines of cinnamon in the shape of a cross, or whatever you like. You can serve it hot, but I think it is better cold.

M'hencha (Moroccan
almond snake)

MUHALLABEYA

Creamed rice pudding   Serves 6

1.2 litres (2 pints) milk

125 g (4 oz) ground rice

150 ml (¼ pint) water,
plus 4 tablespoons

75 g (3 oz) sugar

2–3 tablespoons orange-
flower water or rose-water

3 tablespoons clear honey

75 g (3 oz) mixed almonds
and pistachios, chopped
coarsely

This version of the most common Arab milk pudding
has a honey sauce. The usual one is simply garnished
with nuts; another is baked in the oven.

Bring the milk to the boil. Mix the ground rice
to a paste with the 150 ml (¼ pint) of water
and pour it into the milk, stirring vigorously.
Let it come to the boil again slowly over a very
low heat, stirring all the time so that lumps do
not form (if they do, put the whole thing
through a blender). Cook until the mixture
thickens. Add the sugar and cook, stirring, for
a few minutes longer. Add the orange-flower
water or rose-water and stir well. Pour into a
serving dish and let it cool.

In a pan, mix the honey with the remaining
water and heat until it melts. Leave it to cool.

Pour the syrup over the cold pudding.
Garnish with the nuts and serve.

FAWAKEH

Fruit (Pictured on page 5)

In every country of the Middle East each daily
meal ends with fruit. Often the fruits are cut
up so that guests can sample a variety. Few
things can be as alluring or give as much
pleasure as a large display of fruits of different
textures, flavours, shapes and colours – small
ones left whole, large ones cut in slices or
wedges, some peeled, some not – for people to
pick at. The art lies in cutting them up and
arranging them in the most beautiful manner
possible.

Have an assortment which combines some
common fruits, such as apples, pears, plums,
apricots or greengages, peaches, cherries,
grapes, melon or water melon, with exotic
fruits such as figs, persimmons, dates, mangoes,
prickly pears, paw-paws, guavas, lychees and

pomegranates. Prepare a bowl of water, acidulated with the juice of 1–2 lemons, so that you can drop in the fruits that discolour for a few minutes when you cut them up. Arrange them on a bed of leaves on a very large platter.

'AMAR ELDIN

Apricot dessert   Serves 6

500 g (1 lb) dried apricots

1–2 tablespoons sugar (optional)

125 g (4 oz) blanched almonds, toasted

For the cream:

284 ml (10 fl oz) carton of double cream or thick or strained yogurt

1–2 tablespoons sugar

1 tablespoon orange-flower water or rose-water

Nothing could be easier or more appropriate after a rich meal than this sharp refreshing purée of dried apricots served with a perfumed cream. The most authentic apricots are the slightly acid, orangy-brown, very dry variety; the more usual pale moist kind do not have the same flavour.

Cover the apricots with water and simmer for about 20 minutes or until they are soft and the water is reduced. Put in a blender with the water and purée, adding a little more water if necessary to achieve a smooth cream. Add sugar to taste, if using. Stir in the almonds just before you are ready to serve.

Beat the cream until thick or use the thick or strained yogurt and add the sugar to taste and the orange-flower water or rose-water. Pour over the apricot cream or serve separately.

KHOSHAF

Dried fruit salad   Serves 4

250 g (8 oz) dried apricots

125 g (4 oz) dried prunes

50 g (2 oz) currants or
sultanas

50 g (2 oz) blanched
almonds

1 tablespoon pine kernels

1 tablespoon pistachios, cut
in half

1 tablespoon orange-flower
water or rose-water

*In Turkey they say this dish originates in Anatolia
where, because of its isolation and lack of transport,
the winter diet consists of the summer produce dried
in the sun. Dried prunes, apricots, raisins, apples and
cherries are boiled up in grape juice and served in the
middle of the meal at the same time as rice or bulgar
wheat, beans and meat.*

*But every country has its own version which
depends on the fruits and nuts which grow there. It is
traditionally made during the month of Ramadan
when Muslims fast every day from dawn to sunset.*

Put all the ingredients together in a serving
bowl and leave them to soak in enough water
to cover for 2 days (this gives them a particular
quality). Alternatively, simmer the fruits and
nuts for 25 minutes, adding the flower-water at
the end.

Purée a few of the apricots in a blender with
some of the soaking water and return it to the
bowl to thicken the juice.

Serve chilled.

*Sholezard (Saffron
pudding)
Khoshaf (Dried fruit salad)*

SHOLEZARD

Saffron pudding

2.25 litres (4 pints) water

250 g (8 oz) pudding rice

3 cardamom pods, cracked

250 g (8 oz) sugar

½ teaspoon saffron strands, crushed and mixed with a little water

3 tablespoons rose-water

To garnish:

2 teaspoons ground cinnamon

1 teaspoon finely chopped almonds

1 teaspoon finely chopped pistachios

This delicately coloured and scented rice pudding is Iranian.

Bring the water to the boil in a pan. Throw in the rice and cardamom and cook for 30 minutes. Add the sugar and cook for a further 15 minutes, stirring occasionally.

Add the saffron to the rice and cook for about 30 minutes until the rice has disintegrated into a jelly-like cream. Stir in the rose-water.

Pour into a serving bowl or individual bowls and garnish with the cinnamon, almonds and pistachios, but do not hide all of the brilliant yellow cream. Serve cold.

INDEX TO RECIPES

Cover design: Barry Lowenhoff
Cover illustration: Sally Swabey
Text design: Ken Vail
Photography: Andrew Whittuck
Styling: Bobby Baker
Food preparation for photography: Berit Vinegrad
Illustration: John Woodcock
Typesetting: Ace Filmsetting Ltd, Frome, Somerset
Origination: Colthouse Repro Ltd, Bournemouth
Printed and bound by Printer Trento, Italy